"A thorough and intuitive guide to understanding how money flows in and out of your business. An indispensable must for the start-up or seasonal entrepreneur who wants to grow their business."

—Gino Wickman, Author of *Traction* and *Entrepreneurial Leap*

DISCOVER YOUR FINANCE ENGINE

Leveraging Cash, Profits and Wealth to Secure Sustainable Financial Freedom

DEBRA COOPER

The Finance Engine Series

Published by Author Academy Elite
PO Box 43, Powell, OH 43065
www.AuthorAcademyElite.com

Identifiers:
Library of Congress Control Number: 2020918951
ISBN: 978-1-64746-536-0 (paperback)
ISBN: 978-1-64746-537-7 (hardback)
ISBN: 978-1-64746-538-4 (ebook)

Available in paperback, hardback, e-book, and audiobook

This book is dedicated to all the courageous souls who have embarked on the small business journey with the desire and passion to make the world a better place.

Table of Contents

Note to Reader 3

Introduction 7

Case Study: Sam's Dilemma 11

Part I: The Heart of Your SME

Elusive Road to Success 27

The Embodiment: The What. 31

The Controller: The Who 35

Pulling Back the Skin: The Why. 41

Building Your Empire: The How. 43

No Time like the Present: The When 49

Part 2: The Three Platforms to Financial Freedom

Chapter 1: Without Profits, What's the Point: *The Measure of Your Business* 55

Chapter 2: The Ingredients of Profitability: *Elements of the P&L* 69

Chapter 3: The Blood of Your Entity: *Let's Keep the Blood of Your Business Pumping!* 103

Chapter 4: Without Stability, What's the Point: *When Revenue Streams Fail, Where Are You?* . 117

Chapter 5: The Recipe of Stability: *Elements of the Balance Sheet* 127

Chapter 6: The Backbone of Your Entity: *No Backbone, No Survival* 167

Chapter 7: Without Oxygen, What's the Point: *Cash Makes Your Enterprise Breathe* 189

Chapter 8: The Ingredients of Oxygen: *Elements of the Cash Flow Statement* 199

Chapter 9: The Lifeline of your Entity: *Without Cash Reserves, You Die!* 211

Part 3: Fine Tuning Your Finance Engine

Case Study: Sam's Dilemma Solved 229

Change Your Financial Destiny. 235

Bibliography 239
Acknowledgements 241
About the Author 243
About Zephyr Management Solutions 244
About bizzness breeze essentials 245
Next Steps in Discovering Your SME's Finance Engine . . 247

Happiness is not in the mere possession of money;
it lies in the joy of achievement, in the thrill of creative effort.

—Franklin D. Roosevelt

SME is a universal abbreviation used worldwide to describe the smaller and medium business entities.

Note to Reader

The entrepreneurial journey is not an easy one. It encompasses many learning curves and hills.

From fine turning the unique solution you have created, understanding and implementing marketing strategies and tools, managing the convoluted issues surrounding staff, handling the production process, and designing efficient logistic and distribution strategies to understanding and managing your finances, it is easy to become overwhelmed and disheartened by the challenge.

However, of all the obstacles you face as an entrepreneur, the challenge crucial to your SME's success is financial management.

The aim of *Discover Your Finance Engine* is to provide a quick and easy guide for exploring the financial statements your SME's Finance Engine can produce and how they can add value to the management of your enterprise. Taking into account the characteristics and challenges that the smaller entity faces, I used concepts adopted by big business and modified them into a process the small business entrepreneur can utilize. My ultimate endeavour is to clarify the financial jargon thrown about when discussing finances with professionals and cut to the chase regarding how these financial statements fit within the scope of small business management.

Whether you are new to the entrepreneurial journey or have been managing an SME for some time, you are a traditional bricks and mortar entity or a new age online enterprise, it is always a good time to strengthen your grasp on your SME's Finance Engine. The first step in gaining financial control of your SME is understanding the financial statements your Finance Engine produces.

While all concepts and definitions are consistent with the accounting standards produced by relevant associations in your region and throughout the world, they have not been applied rigidly. Accounting standards ensure uniformity for investors and associations external to your SME. The objective of this book is to provide the SME owner, no matter which region they operate within, an understanding of their own financial statements so they can format them to support their internal decision making.

This self-help guide assumes the reader has limited to no knowledge of business finances. This has allowed me to start at the roots of business terms and concepts, so I can take you on the journey to *Discover Your Finance Engine*. Though anyone can benefit, this guide is for the beginner in SME financial management who wishes to better understand how money flows in and out of their SME, and to improve the management of their Finance Engine and capitalisation of the information it provides.

Be warned! You will not become a financial expert on your SME's financial statements by a simple skimming of this guide. You may need to read through it several times and occasionally refer back to previous sections as you review your own SME's financial statements from one month to the next.

The objective is to help you understand how these statements should look and highlight any shortcomings. Over time, as each reporting period passes, you will be better able to absorb and implement changes to the statements to improve the management of your finances and your small business.

Thank you for investing in *Discover Your Finance Engine–Leveraging Cash, Profits and Wealth to Secure Sustainable Financial Freedom*. I hope you find value in the coming pages. If, by the final page, I have improved your mindset regarding the value of your entity's Finance Engine, then I have achieved my objective.

Wishing you prosperity in all your small business endeavours with kind regards,

Debra Cooper

Introduction

"So, you are an entrepreneur. Great! And you want to grow your business activity and create a sustainable business around your entrepreneurial concept? Terrific! So, what's your current financial position?"

"I have no idea, not until I send my books to my tax accountant,"

Or,

"I'm behind with my bookkeeping, several months in fact. However, last time I checked everything was fine."

Every time I hear a comment like these, I hear warning bells.

To build a successful, sustainable and profitable business, an entrepreneur must UNDERSTAND, MANAGE and OWN the Finance Engine of their SME. If they do not, it is entrepreneurial SUICIDE.

I frequently hear SME business owners complain about the burden of keeping their bookkeeping current. They do not view this function as a revenue producing activity, so give it low priority, and push it aside until the eve of financial or taxation deadlines when they demand attention. This behaviour is to the detriment of the entrepreneur and their business.

The SME's Finance Engine should be seen as a cash-producing asset, similar to an employee would be to a service-based business or a manufacturing machine that produces the products you sell. When the Finance Engine's mechanics are understood, managed and owned by the entrepreneur, this function becomes a reliable and intuitive asset the SME cannot survive without. Not only are you in a position to minimise your business costs and leverage off the small wins in revenue earnings generated from your marketing engine, you can manage your business to maximise profit levels, entrench your financial stability and accumulate cash reserves to survive that eventual rainy day.

This is a crucial step if you are serious about growing your business into an entity that is sustainable in the long term and will provide you with financial freedom. Taking these steps will not only add value to you and your staff, but to your customers, suppliers and business partners. You must take ownership of your SME's Finance Engine.

One way you can take control of your finances is by driving the process of completing and updating your accounting records, instead of waiting for external parties to push you into the task. When you manage your finances to self-imposed and concise deadlines, you keep your pulse on the results of your business activity. You will extract gems of information hidden in your Finance Engine that will improve your SME management and shore up the chances of success.

Sound promising?

If you are ready to convert your mindset about financial management from a weighted burden into an invaluable and informative asset, you have made a great start by investing in *Discover Your Finance Engine*. This is the first self-help guidebook in the 'Finance Engine' series that aims to clarify the three core financial statements, their purpose and what they say about your business.

We will outline a case study for Sam's Landscaping & Design. The case study is used throughout the guide to provide examples of common situations that the SME faces and to clarify concepts and elements that relate to the three core financial statements. When reviewing the case study examples, look at your own respective financial statements. As these statements encompass your entity's business activity, our discussion will further clarify the concepts and elements and how they apply directly to you.

In part one we look at the what, who, why, how and when of the three core financial statements and how they relate to your SME's Finance Engine. We will outline your role as the entrepreneur / business owner and what level of reporting your SME should prepare at a minimum.

In part two, we discuss each of the three core financial statements. We will outline the purpose and importance of each statement, the elements they report upon, and each element's relationship with others reported on the statement. This section will also cover the relationship of each statement with the other two core statements and how you can preserve their health and, subsequently, the health of your SME.

In part three, we outline the next steps in taking ownership of your SME's Finance Engine, and shoring up your business' chances of sustainability and longevity to achieve financial freedom.

By the end of this self-help guide you should be able to:

1. Identify the three core financial statements;

2. Identify, understand and interpret the elements reported on each financial statement;

3. Understand and interpret the relationship of each element with others on the financial statement;

4. Understand the relationship between the three core financial statements;

5. Be able to identify discrepancies, losses and wins in the elements reported;

6. Be in an informed and empowered position to manage your SME's Finance Engine.

I aim to provide a self-help guide for the busy entrepreneur that is concise, factual and easy to read at the end of a long day, while inspiring you to take ownership of your SME's Finance Engine and your financial freedom.

Case Study
Sam's Dilemma

The case study scenario is based on a fictional company and depicts a turning point for Sam's Landscaping & Design. The business owner is forced to face the truth about how he is managing his SME's Finance Engine and the impact this has on his business. The dilemma and repercussions Sam faces represent my experience working with small business and will provide realistic examples to clarify the elements and concepts discussed.

*Please note, Sam's Landscaping & Design is an entirely fictional business used for demonstrative purposes only. Any reference or resemblance to an existing business or businesses is purely accidental.

The case study begins when the business owner, Sam Buchan, receives news that has a detrimental financial impact on his business.

Sam Buchan hurled his phone into the corner. It slammed into the filing cabinet with a deafening thud; the vibrations echoed throughout the room and into his heart.

Sam's breath caught in his throat, and pain ripped through his chest. He pressed his hand to his stomach as it cartwheeled, threatening to return his last meal. After a thirty second phone call, everything he had worked for during the past five years crumbled around him. He desperately tried sorting through the implications, but it was too much to absorb all at once. Jake's news kept replaying in his mind.

His wife, Beth, appeared just inside the doorway. She had been out to lunch with her girlfriends yet again, her cheeks still pink from the wine and ambient exuberance of the gathering. The couple had their weekly argument that morning as they tried to work out how they would finance the payroll. She initially glided into the office on a wave of euphoria, but the greyness of concern now shadowed her blue eyes. How was he going to tell her what Jake's news meant for them, for their business…for their way of life?

"What on Earth was that? You look like you're going to be sick," she said. She eyed the abandoned phone laying lifeless on the floor, separated from its case during the collision.

"Our business," Sam mumbled, unable to continue.

Beth sat down opposite him and ran her fingers through her long blonde hair, toying with the curls like she always did when she was worried or uneasy. "What do you mean, our business?"

"Jake." Sam croaked, his voice failing him. He needed to show confidence that everything would be ok. "Jake," he said again, his voice stronger. "He called in the loan."

Beth's gaze hardened. "The loan that we never ever had to pay back."

"He has to declare it. He'll need the money to settle the divorce."

"You mean, Suzie's making him cash it in." There was no love lost between her and her sister. "She never agreed with it." Beth picked up his mobile and the discarded case, placing them on his

desk. She rested her hands on her hips, preparing to fight. "Well, we simply can't pay it. I've just had to beg Sally at Benefit Homes to pay some of their invoices early. $200,000 is going to be a little harder to find."

"We have no choice. Suzie is hitting Jake up for seventy percent and his solicitor says that while they'll fight it, she's likely to win. Jake doesn't have the cash to cover it himself, and that money is legally his."

"So, we have to suffer because my sister wants out." Beth's voice rose with each word. "Maybe we can ask your dad?" she suggested, grasping the wings of desperation.

"Like hell I'm asking him. He just coughed up sixty grand for the land we bought in March for the second yard. This is our problem and we will fix it. Even if it means selling the house," he added with conviction, knowing this statement would ignite her fury.

Beth didn't disappoint. Her tirade started with the lack of reward for her years of support and ended with the pride and love she had for the dream home they had built two years ago that they just completed furnishing. As usual, she failed to see the contradiction in her argument.

Sam let her vent. There was no point fuelling the fire. As expected, the blaze finally burnt down to a blubber of tears, but he was no better dealing with her in this state.

"What are we going to do?" She hiccupped as she fell into the chair, defeated.

"I don't know."

"Maybe, you should call Frank."

"No. Every time I speak with him, I end up in a group call with five other accountants on his team, followed by a bill for a couple thousand dollars after they've only told me what do rather than give me the support I'm paying for. Besides, we still owe him that twenty grand, and he's unlikely to be forthcoming without payment and further cost."

"The bank? Pete McPherson might be able to help."

"A bank loan? Beth, the repayments would kill us. The beauty about Jake's loan is that it's interest only and at a rate below the market rate in this economy."

"Sam, please. Can't you talk to the bank before you sell our house? I couldn't bear it."

He hated to admit it, but Beth was right. A bank loan was their only chance of dealing with this quickly. But it was only transferring the problem to a more demanding and rigid financier. Jake had always been accommodating when they couldn't meet his interest repayments. The bank wouldn't be.

"How long have you got?" Beth was already distancing herself from the problem.

"Until the 30th of June. Five—no, six—weeks away."

Beth stood and brushed down the front of her shirt like she was trying to remove the bad taste of this news as though they were wrinkles. She was leaving it to him to solve this dilemma, and the thought sent a tidal wave of anxiety through him.

"I'll make an appointment with the bank for you. Friday morning would be best since Tom can handle the Fraser job without you," she said before leaving.

He wondered if she truly realised the impact this was going to have. Despite managing the business' finances, she did not seem to grasp the severity of their situation. That, or she thought ignoring it would make it go away. Sam had trouble understanding it himself; on paper and according to their tax bill, it looked like they had a solid, viable business. Meanwhile, the lack of cash was crippling them. It just didn't make any sense.

Sam considered the option of selling the house. It would set them right again and they could go forward without having to finance a business loan. But they would then be without a home. He shook his head to rid himself of the next thought.

If he sold her house, he would be heading for divorce next.

Sam woke in a pool of sweat. The bright glow of 2:44 am stared at him from the alarm clock. He listened to the rhythm of Beth breathing next to him. Slow. Deliberate. Excruciatingly at peace.

Unable to tolerate his wife's carefree sleep, he got out of bed, threw on his beloved tracksuit and went downstairs to the bar-room to pour himself a Jamieson whisky. It would be awhile before he'd be able to buy another so he'd have to make this bottle last. The thought made him slump to the floor, a glass in one hand and the bottle in the other, back propped up against the wall.

But how long would 'a while' be?

Sam wanted the world to cave in upon him and make everything go away. The past few days had been unbearable.

His eye caught the portrait of his wife and three kids, hanging on the wall opposite him. It was barely a year old and whilst he recognised the family as his own, they felt disconnected and foreign, existing outside of the bubble that enclosed him. His relationship had been strongest with his eldest, Max, aged eight, yet he could not remember the last time they'd spoken other than with an instruction or a 'not now' rebuttal. Six-year-old Tyler showed signs of being as flighty as his mother, a characteristic that grated Sam's nerves as he suffocated in his hour of need. His gaze drifted to Oakley, the youngest at four, and Sam realised he barely knew him, unable to recall his favourite toy or colour. He could very well be someone else's kid.

The image of Beth standing behind the kids towered over Sam as he slid further into the floor. He failed to make the appointment due to work commitments and was omitted from the family portrait entirely. Despite the smile on Beth's lips, there was a glint in her eye, forever disciplining him for his absence. No doubt that was the reason she insisted they hang the finished product in the room that was his. A constant reminder of his neglect.

It had been a long time since he'd done anything right in Beth's eyes, and for months, their frustrations ricocheted off of one another, feeding the demise descending upon them. They only spoke about the business these days and, more often than not, the conversations escalated into a scrabble of heated words and emotions. He couldn't remember when he last touched her or when she had reached for him. It was the beginning of the end, of that he was certain.

Sam had to find a solution, but he was at a loss for where to start. The burden in that moment was so heavy he couldn't even stand.

For the past week, every time he did or said anything, he did so with the black essence of doom wrapped around him. It was like being an imposter living in someone else's skin, unable to control the downward spiral. Each moment suffocated him so relentlessly that bringing himself to think of the next took unsurmountable energy and willpower. When the next moment inevitably arrived, he was hesitant to take a breath. But he had to—he had to keep on breathing and working. He must keep pushing forward, for there were so many people dependent upon him: his wife, kids, employees, customers, suppliers, Frank, the Bank, and Jake.

Three days after Jake's impenetrable phone call, he realised his situation went far deeper than he'd believed. The surrounding support was frivolous in his time of need. A phone call to Frank only confirmed his fears, as the accountant diplomatically requested payment before he addressed Sam's newest mess. The bank was equally unhelpful.

Sam's visit that Friday had not gone well. Pete McPherson was no longer with the bank, forcing Sam to meet with his incumbent, a twenty-year-old boy set on following the bank's procedures to the letter. They went through the initial steps of investigating Sam's ability to finance such a loan, discussed how long it would take and what he needed to provide to proceed with the application. For a moment he was at peace, with an end to the crippling effect of Jake's decision finally at hand. It didn't last.

"We will just need a full set of financials to proceed. If you can get them to us by next Friday, we will have no problem meeting your deadline," the boy said, his lack of sympathy apparent in every word.

Sam left the bank and stood fastened to the nature strip as if his feet were set into the concrete. Not only would he have to jump a hundred hurdles to meet the bank's application requirement, the foreboding that accompanied the five years of repayments he would need to find the money for threatened to derail him.

The world was against him.

What on Earth had he done so wrong, to face losing everything, when everything had started off so well? How could this have happened?

Their small business journey started with a bang. Sam, after a couple years of deliberation, finally made the jump five years ago. It was Jake, his brother-in-law, who had provided the most encouragement. He not only provided a substantial loan to purchase the plant and equipment, but he also referred several large landscaping projects to the new company. It was a perfect start as the stars fell into alignment for every new project.

Those first jobs soon developed into a steady stream of residential landscaping jobs riding on the wave of referrals. Within six months, they settled into a steady schedule where he was consistently booked weeks in advance. He employed a fully trained landscaper and several apprentices at various levels of experience to establish his first team. Sam was on his way up and it had been so seamless that he often wondered why he'd procrastinated taking the leap.

The start-up years were ideal. He concentrated on providing both soft and hard landscaping to the residential market and got most of his future work through customer referrals and local radio advertising. Whilst he provided the professional designs and subsequent quotes for each customer himself, his head landscaper served as team leader onsite. This enabled Sam the freedom of visiting current sites to assess them for quality assurance, visit future sites to facilitate quoting and keeping the schedule full with a steady stream of projects. He organised materials and equipment each job required and ensured his team was on track to complete each project on time.

Two years ago, he joined forces with a property developer who specialised in providing turnkey investment properties, Thrifty Investments. They needed a landscaper to design and construct the landscapes for their suite of house plans. Sam couldn't believe his luck as this was guaranteed recurring and structured work year-round. He set up two additional teams, dedicated to constructing these landscapes.

Overnight his business doubled in size, and the initial momentum was intoxicating. A barrage of issues developed daily, and they spent most of their time problem-solving the constant cycle of issues. It took twelve months to grow accustomed to this escalated momentum, and soon the frantic state was the norm.

If Sam was honest with himself, that was about the time the cash started drying up, though he didn't know why. Sam did all the quoting himself, always ensuring that at least a forty percent mark-up was applied and that the sales invoices were raised at the commencement of jobs to ensure they could capture all the payments they received. Beth dealt with everything else. She managed the payroll, paid the suppliers and the loan instalments, and processed all the associated transactions into an accounting database. She even set up bank feeds that saved her heaps of time and ensured all transactions were recorded.

Occasionally, Beth would provide Sam with a Profit & Loss Statement and it always reported a good profit. In fact, he couldn't remember seeing a loss at all in recent years, even during the low seasonal months. It didn't make any sense that they never had cash. Their profitability was consistently good, however the only consistency about their bank balance was that they almost never had one. Sam had to summon courage to check the balance, fearful it was never enough. More often than not, it wasn't.

Every week was a scramble to find enough cash to cover the team's wages; Sam doubted the boys stayed out of loyalty anymore. Dealing with the employees was a constant juggle, managing their complaints about the jobs they got stuck on and the hours they worked, and showing their disdain when Sam insisted upon rework to get a job up to scratch. It'd been months since they shared a beer at the pub or since Sam had made any effort to check on their personal wellbeing. No, they didn't stay out of loyalty anymore. If they didn't get paid, they wouldn't show.

Before the dream home, Beth would draw down on the excess funds in their mortgage when they needed to prop up the business' bank balance. However, this option was no longer available since they built their extravagant home. They met the minimum mortgage repayments by the skin of their teeth, and for most months they couldn't draw a wage from the business at all. To meet the payroll bill, they developed an unhealthy reliance on calling in invoices that were not yet due.

His only saving grace was Thrifty Investments. Not only the business they provided him, but their willingness to make payment ahead of the due date when requested. His relationship with Wayne was so solid that they were increasing the workload to include the western suburbs of Melbourne, which required two more teams, and were undertaking initial talks about expanding into the northern suburbs the following year. However, all of this expansion and growth needed cash—cash they didn't have.

Sam took another swig from the whisky bottle, the glass abandoned beside him. For days his mind had been cycling through the past five years until he had exhausted every detail he could remember, dissected every possibility he could utilise. Not only could Sam not see the answer, he just didn't have the energy to look for it anymore.

At eight am his wife found him behind the bar, curled into the foetal position, hugging the empty whisky bottle. If he hadn't passed out, he would have seen the look of disdain on her face.

In desperation, Sam visited his father. He wouldn't ask for another loan, but he needed a sounding board from someone who had been in the same game most of his life. Whilst even his dad couldn't

hand him a solution on a silver platter, he suggested Sam talk to Jake to see if they could come up with another solution before committing himself to Frank and the Bank, or doing the unthinkable and selling his wife's dream home.

Unwilling to go home and face Beth and the kids, Sam and his dad went to the local pub and had a counter meal he couldn't afford. By the time his father left him, he had set up a meeting with Jake later that afternoon at the same establishment, and was feeling a little better about his self-worth, even if it was only a shadow. Whilst he waited for Jake, he headed to the bar and ordered an orange juice.

The publican was a fellow he'd gone to school with. They'd never been friends, but they always exchanged pleasantries when, in the distant past, Sam and the boys had dropped in after a hard day's work. The publican placed the drink on the bar while an amused smirk curled his lips.

"Been awhile. Looks like you've seen better days," Paul's voice boomed, cutting through the noise.

"Yeah, you could say that."

Paul busied himself with other patrons without another word. When they finished their beverages and moved to a table in the opposite direction, Paul returned to Sam. He crossed over his arms and rested them on the bar top at a respectable, but confiding distance.

"What's up?"

Sam wasn't usually one to speak about his finances, but he confided in Paul; that's what bartenders are for, right? It was mostly a way to get a handle on his anxiety before the meeting with Jake. He wasn't expecting a solution to present itself, so he wasn't in a receptive state of mind when Paul, wordlessly, handed over a business card.

"Give my bookkeeper a call. She'll sort you out."

"Bookkeeper? No thanks, I've heard of the problems they can cause. I'm in deep enough without handing over the books so she can make the mess bigger."

"This one's different. Since I took her on, I've learned more about my business' finances than I ever knew existed. Debra not only showed me where the problems were, but she worked with me to get them fixed. Now my bank account is always flush and I know exactly where I am. Not to mention that my tax accountant's bill is a lot smaller than it once was.

"We're building a three-year plan on how to increase my seating capacity by renovating the adjoining yard into a beer garden, and I'm financing it all with internal funds."

"I don't need a three-year plan. I need a now plan," Sam said. Jealousy that Paul had it all together reared its ugly head.

"Contact her. You'd be a fool not to. She won't charge you for an initial consultation and she'll be up front if she can't help you. Sounds like you have nothing to lose."

"Only my entire business."

"Aren't you losing that anyway?"

Sam pinched his lips into a frown. Paul left to solve the problems of another patron while Sam put the business card in his top pocket and resumed wallowing in his orange juice. Paul's words joined his swirling thoughts until Jake arrived. Sam bought them each a beer and they moved to a quiet corner.

As they settled in, Sam assessed Jake's receptiveness. He was in bad shape. His shirt was half tucked into a pair of pants that looked recently unravelled from a tightly constrained ball. His skin was sallow, deep black indentations underlined each eye, and his usually manicured hair was unruly and in need of a good wash. Even though he forced a smile, it lacked his usual confidence.

It was like looking in a mirror.

Jake apologised for his appearance, and they sat in silence drinking their beers. Sam realised that no matter what crisis he was in, he still had his family. Jake had lost his and was on the brink of losing a whole lot more. Sam briefly touched the card in his top pocket.

"So, what did you want to discuss?" Jake asked.

"I just wanted to see how you were doing?" Sam said, unable to place more burden on Jake's shoulders. He was family, the only family Jake had left, and surely that meant he had to be more supportive than Frank and the Bank had been to him.

"There's no problem with the loan?"

"Not yet. I'm still making inquiries," Sam said, finding some self-assurance and gratitude that he could help ease Jake's situation, at least for the time being. "More importantly, how are you doing?"

Relief relaxed Jake's features as his eyebrows unfurled and the tension in his shoulders relaxed. It was like an antidote to the hangover Sam carried over the insolvability of his problem. It shouted that there was hope.

Against Beth's wishes, Sam took Paul's suggestion and contacted the bookkeeper, Debra. The three of them discussed the extent of the situation encompassing the need to repay the interest-only loan, the timeframe and them not having enough capital to pay it outright without refinancing. Sam was too embarrassed to highlight the extent of his cash flow issues and Beth, in her unwillingness to embrace the bookkeeper's assistance, also made no mention of it.

The bookkeeper explained she could get the financial statements in a condition that should satisfy the bank. If the bank required Frank's endorsement, she assured them it would be only a formality because she would guarantee the books would be clean. With a quick glance at the bank statements, she offered them a flat price to get them into shape, which was much less than what Frank would have charged. Even though it was the bookkeeper's diplomacy managing his wife's derision that convinced Sam.

Before Debra left, she handed over a book titled, Discover Your Finance Engine, asking Sam and his wife to read it.

"Once I have your books fully reconciled, we will sit down and review the financial statements in detail. This guide book will help us get the most out of our next meeting."

Like a gentle breeze, the bookkeeper was gone, and they settled into the day's frantic rhythm.

It couldn't be that easy, could it?

Part 1

The Heart of Your SME

Elusive Road to Success

WHEN YOU EMBARK upon the small business journey, you focus on the gift you are contributing to the world.

This gift encompasses the unique solution you have created that solves a problem near and dear to your heart. You are driven by passion and are fulfilled when you help someone who is facing the very problem your gift solves. When fuelled by this passion and success during these initial weeks or months, there is often little mention of money.

Whilst there is usually a level of expectation that you can commercialise your gift, it is not the driving motivation for the most successful of businesses. Offering your gift to the world and making someone else's life easier is the primary objective. Unfortunately, this is where the quandary lies. For a business to reach the heights of success and be sustainable in the long term, prudent financial management is mandatory.

For the impassioned entrepreneur, managing their SME's finances is less critical than ensuring customer satisfaction, their staff are happy, and ancillary issues are resolved swiftly. Many new business owners don't manage their finances beyond their SME's bank account, ensuring only that there is enough cash to pay the month's expenditures or even just the following week's commitments.

When starting out, the financial education of many SME entrepreneurs starts and ends with managing the household check book. They think this skill set transfers to the management of their SME's finances, not realizing the complexities involved. The business finances and intimate movements of money in and out of an SME are more far-reaching than household financial management and can quickly get out of hand.

The SME's Finance Engine is, more often than not, viewed as a burden—a time-consuming task that pulls their attention away from generating sales and servicing their customer base. Deadlines provided by third party stakeholders end up driving the entrepreneur to update their SME's Finance Engine at the last minute, causing them to miss out on vital financial information and opportunities.

More businesses fail from financial mismanagement than for any other reason. Not only do aspiring entrepreneurs start their small business journey with insufficient capital, but the management of the capital they generate is often managed poorly. Throughout my experiences working with and within the smaller entity, many viable businesses never get the chance to succeed because there is a lack of focus on the financial flows in and around their businesses. The Finance Engine and the benefits it provides are often undervalued and underutilised, making the road to success unnecessarily challenging, or even impassable.

The Finance Engine of your SME is as unique as your business model, the problem you are trying to solve, and the solution you're delivering to the market. Survival depends on the SME entrepreneur understanding the intimate mechanics of their Finance Engine and how this function, when managed properly, can be an invaluable asset to managing their business.

If you are serious about growing your SME into a vibrant and sustainable entity, you need to jump on the learning curve to *Discover your Finance Engine* and the three core financial statements it produces. The earlier you can educate yourself in your entrepreneurial journey, the easier and quicker the path will be towards a financially successful SME. Even for the seasoned entrepreneur, it is never too late to develop a more thorough understanding of your SME's Finance Engine. When your accounting records are up to-date and accurate, they can provide you with a sound summary of your SME's business activity and identify gems of information that can improve and simplify the management of your SME.

The Embodiment: The What

What constitutes your SME's Finance Engine?

When I refer to your SME's Finance Engine, I am discussing the financial function of your business. A characteristic of an engine is to propel you forward. When you have structured your financial function to run efficiently, it adds value to your business, thus propelling your business forward.

Well-managed finance functions capture all business records in an accurate, timely and consistent manner. This streamlines the flow of monies in and out of your entity and provides financial information about your business activity that empowers the decision-making and management of your SME.

The three core financial statements organise your SME's financial data into an intuitive and informative format that supports you in making effective decisions on allocating your

SME's resources to achieve profitability and financial stability for the long-term.

The three core financial statements are:

- Profit & Loss Statement;
- Balance Sheet; and
- Cash Flow Statement.

The Profit & Loss Statement, often referred to as the P&L, is the most commonly understood by the SME entrepreneur. It reports on the earnings from daily business activity and will discern whether your SME is making a profit or losing money.

The Balance Sheet is less familiar, but is more important. It reports on the financial stability of your SME by summarising your business model's resources. When your Profit & Loss Statement fails to produce profits, it is the Balance Sheet that will determine whether your SME will survive and for how long.

The Cash Flow Statement is often overlooked, yet it is the most important statement. It provides a summary of the cash transactions that run through your business and reports on which business activities your SME's cash is being allocated to. It can explain the *why*, when your SME's seemingly healthy profits are not converting into cash reserves.

Each of these statements serves an individual purpose in isolation of the other two. However, together they can provide layers of financial information about your SME's business activity. Before you can effectively and efficiently leverage your SME on this information, you need an understanding of each statement's purpose, the elements they are reporting on and what circumstances describe a statement as healthy.

"But who has time to prepare these reports?"

Regarding unrelenting time constraints and your SME's valuable cash reserves, the true question should be, "*Who can afford not to*?"

The Controller: The Who

Which SMEs Should Prepare the Three Core Financial Statements?

SME's vary in size and form and will vary regarding resources, capital, labour, cash, and even time. Preparing and maintaining the three core financial statements requires an investment of each of these resources. This makes the task more cumbersome for smaller SMEs who have greater resource constraints.

The definition of an SME across the world varies marginally from one country to the next, taking into account the number of staff and annual revenue or total assets of the entity to classify them. For this guide, we have defined the SME as follows:

- ***Micro SME***—an entity that has up to 4 employees.

- ***Small SME***—an entity that has between 5 and 19 employees.
- ***Medium SME***—an entity that has between 20 and 200 employees.

Today, with the opportunities provided by technology and the internet, it is foreseeable that a micro entity can generate revenue levels that were once only enjoyed by medium or larger businesses. The number of employees is more indicative of an SME's business structure complexity, the level of resources available to them and the capability of these resources. The resources mirror the complexity, size and capability of the SME's Finance Engine.

The cost for a micro SME to prepare the books, and subsequently prepare fully reconciled financial statements, is often in excess of the benefits gained. At the other extreme, the medium SME will lose out on gems of information about their business if they only produce one of the three financial statements.

I recommend the following *minimums* regarding which financial statements a SME with moderating business activity should be preparing.

- ***Micro SME***—Cash Flow Statement only.
- ***Small SME***—Profit & Loss Statement and Cash Flow Statement.
- ***Medium SME***—All three core financial statements.

The micro SME implementing aggressive growth strategies and seeking to grow a sustainable entity for the long-term would benefit from preparing the three financial statements from the outset. Tracking your growing business activity will allow you to develop an understanding of the financial impact of your decisions, and guide and support decisions you implement. There is invaluable, intuitive information that can be gained from preparing all three financial statements, which is lost when only one or two of the statements are prepared. By utilizing all three financial statements from the beginning, the micro entity will become intimately familiar with the financial workings of the SME, making maintenance substantially simpler.

Who Should Prepare the Three Core Financial Statements?

As the owner of an SME, you have a responsibility to be abreast of your business activities and ensure you can drive your business forward. The most effective way to achieve this is to be ahead of the financial impact of your business' activities.

More often than not, your perception of how profitable a project or specific business activity is will differ from the actual profitability. When an activity is not measured and subsequently managed by perception, it can quickly burn through your cash, despite it appearing profitable. It is imperative to review your financials on a regular basis.

Your SME's Finance Engine encapsulates three tasks:

- ***Data Entry***—entering of your business transactions into a database that converts the data into usable information.
- ***Reconciliation***—verification of the transactions entered via data entry are accurate, consistent and up-to date.
- ***Analysis***—interrogation of the information produced by the reconciled transactions.

Mismanagement occurs when the business owner spends their time processing transactions into a database. Not only is it a time-consuming task, it is often repetitive. While many start out performing the bookkeeping task, once the volume of transactions reaches a level that imposes upon your time or capabilities, appoint a qualified professional to manage your business transactions.

A professional can process your transactions accurately and as close to the end of a reporting period as possible, preparing a set of fully reconciled financial statements whilst meeting your statutory tax commitments. They have experience in the field and can perform the tasks more accurately and efficiently than you can while occupied with other business duties.

You can hire professional bookkeepers to prepare your books as infrequently as a quarterly basis. When your business activity increases and the function becomes more arduous to stay abreast of, you may employ a part-time or full-time bookkeeper directly. When considering a bookkeeper to prepare your books and the three core financial statements, ensure you verify certificate qualifications.

There is a significant difference between someone who has data entry skills and one who has accredited bookkeeping skills.

Difference between Data Entry and Bookkeeping

While many people think bookkeeping and data entry are the same, each of these functions serve a different purpose and, more importantly, require distinct skill sets.

Data entry is the process of entering data into an organised system, usually computerised. As it applies to your SME's finances, data entry refers only to the processing of your business' transactions into a computerised database.

As technology becomes more sophisticated, current accounting software is becoming more automated. Transactions can be entered into the database via direct data links with your financial institution and can be recorded with minimal accounting knowledge. However, the business owner that believes that this function can encapsulate their entire bookkeeping function does so to their business' detriment.

Whilst bookkeeping can incorporate data entry, the core purpose of its function is to reconcile. Reconciliation is the process that converts data entered into an organized database into meaningful information.

At this stage, you can use the reconciled data with a level of assurance in making more informed and sound decisions in managing your business. When an accounting database has been fully reconciled, you can rely on the three financial statements to be accurate. Without reconciliation, data can be misleading and incomplete, resulting in mislead decisions that could harm your SME.

Reconciliation is not a skill that everyone possesses. However, it is an essential skill required for every bookkeeper and accountant and is the difference between a data entry operator and a bookkeeper. It is imperative for the bookkeeper to fully reconcile your business transactions before the three financial statements are prepared. Many business owners know the bank account requires reconciliation daily, or at bare minimum, at the end of the month. This process should be applied to all elements reported on the financial statements.

For instance, revenue needs to be reconciled to ensure all sales made during a period have been captured. Inventory balances need reconciliation to ensure the inventory levels in the database accurately reflect what is physically held on a shop floor. Accounts Receivables need to be reconciled to ensure your financial statements reflect the correct value of customer invoices that are outstanding, and Accounts Payables to ensure all supplier invoices and associated expenses have been captured and processed. This includes loan accounts, credit card accounts, prepaid expenses, prepaid deposits and so on.

Only once all elements on the three financial statements are reconciled in full can the financial statements provide the reader with an accurate picture of where their business stands.

Responsibility of the Entrepreneur

Time is a valuable resource of the SME entrepreneur who must allocate it wisely. As a business owner, you will be more productive by delegating responsibility of data entry and bookkeeping. You can then invest your time in driving your business and scrutinizing your financial statements, instead of preparing them.

When your Finance Engine is set up correctly to produce fully reconciled financial statements and you understand the elements they report upon, analysis can take as little as one hour per month. In that hour you will have verified which areas of your business need your immediate attention, which activities you should discard, and which wins are humming along on track with your expectations.

Pulling Back the Skin: The Why

PART TWO IS dedicated to answering *the why*, but we will touch upon it here.

The overarching benefit of understanding your Finance Engine and the three core financial statements is to support your decision-making and improve your effectiveness in small business management. When your accounting records are up to-date, accurate and provide a comprehensive financial summary of your business, the benefits include, but are not limited to, the provision of:

- Up-to-date and intimate information about your business activities,
- Identifying the areas of your business which are and are not profitable,
- Isolating activities that add to your cash balance,

- Pinpointing activities that burn your cash resources,
- Diagnosing why some activities that reap healthy profits are not boosting your cash balance,
- Analysing the financial stability that supports your business activity,
- Identifying the level of debt your SME owes to third parties, and
- Highlighting the amount and implications of drawings you take from your business.

The above list is only a start. In Part Two, we will further discuss each individual statement's purpose and the elements they report upon.

Building Your Empire: The How

WHETHER YOU ARE managing a micro, small or medium SME, you should be capturing the impact of your business activity and reviewing it on a regular basis. But just how regularly?

In the early days of the start-up SME you should, at minimum, be reviewing the monthly business' bank statement to ensure that all transactional movements are genuine and meet with your expectations.

When the volume of transactions increases, each of these transactions should be recorded in an organised system, such as a cash book. Each is then allocated to a specific description, enabling you to determine the sum value of similar nature transactions. While the three core financial statements can be prepared from a cash book, when the volume of transactions becomes cumbersome and time-consuming, turn to technology.

A sophisticated approach is to process all business activity into an accounting database that can generate financial statements. The off-the-shelf accounting software products available today are not only extremely cost effective but are extensive in the value they provide in capturing your data quickly and producing the three core financial statements. Each statement is usually available in a standard format and can be customised to your business.

Cash vs Accrual Accounting

When you use an accounting database to capture your business activity, you will need to understand the method used to record transactions and subsequently, the method that applies to the three core financial statements. Understanding this is crucial to deciphering the information reported for each element.

There are two accounting methods:

- Cash Basis of accounting, or;
- Accrual Basis of accounting.

The Cash Basis of accounting records your business transactions at the time the cash transaction occurs. For example, the date cash is received for a sale is the date it will be recognised and reported under revenue on the Profit & Loss Statement. But if you raise a sales invoice on a date other than when the cash receipt is received, it will not be recognised or reported in the P&L Statement until the date that cash is transferred.

With the Accrual Basis of accounting, transactions are recorded when you raise the invoice. For example, when a customer invoice is raised, the value will be recognised as revenue and reported on the Profit & Loss Statement at the invoice date, whether or not the cash has been received. If the sale does not produce an invoice and cash was received for that sale, it is then recorded at the date that cash was received.

It is important to understand with which accounting basis your financial statements have been prepared. Under the Cash Basis, the values reported against the elements will be different to those prepared under the Accrual Basis. One method is not necessarily better than the other, but it is imperative to understand the difference. When you are reviewing an element on a financial statement, you can interpret how the amounts and totals have been calculated.

SME owners usually start out capturing their transactions on a Cash Basis. However, as the SME's activity becomes more sophisticated, they are likely to migrate to the Accrual Basis of accounting. At the beginning, many owners only record transactions when they appear on their bank statement. Over time, recording of transactions will also become more sophisticated. Once a SME is raising customer invoices, processing supplier invoices and managing inventory through their accounting database, they will probably use the Accrual Basis for better control.

Accounting software packages today are equipped to prepare the financial statements on both the cash and accrual methods. We will look at the difference between Cash Basis and Accrual Basis in more detail when we visit the elements of each financial statement.

Effective Financial Statements

Before the three core financial statements are ready to be analysed, they must be in a condition that supports important business decisions. Only when the statements are in top-notch condition, can we describe them as being effective. But how do we achieve this?

To be effective, the three financial statements need to meet three specific criteria: timely, accuracy and consistency.

- **Timely**

Timeliness of the financial statements refers to when they are prepared. For the statements to be timely you need to compile them as close to the end of the reporting period as possible. The later you prepare the statements after the reporting period, the later any decisions can be made on the information reported, which delays subsequent action that can drastically affect your SME's finances. This becomes critical when you wish to stop a financially compromising position before it goes further. On the other side, you can also leverage your successes as early as possible.

For the average SME, statements should be prepared no later than the fifth business day of the following month. This will allow analysis and investigation of the information close enough to the end of the reporting period that any subsequent action can be taken when the new reporting period's business activity is still in its early stages. You can take advantage of the successes you identified and will find yourself in a better position to stem problems before they carry forward into another reporting period.

It can be challenging to prepare your statements within this time period. Though our ability to control the processing of transactions such as sales and cash payments will allow us to process them as close to occurrence as possible, receiving supplier invoices or other documents from external third-parties can add to that difficulty.

You may need to negotiate with these external parties to request such documents earlier so you can process them in the correct reporting period. Not only will this allow you to prepare and close your books as soon as possible, but you can ensure they are accurate.

- **Accuracy**

The three financial statements are considered accurate once fully reconciled. This means you have processed every transaction that has physically occurred during the reporting period. Reconciliation serves as a check that every transaction is captured and accurate.

For example, by reconciling the bank account, you ensure all cash transactions are processed and the balance in your accounting records is the same as what the bank reports.

Every element of the three core financial statements should be reconciled. By having procedures in place, you can conduct this activity in a timely fashion and have faith you can rely on the prepared statements for making decisions.

While it is a statutory requirement for tax or accounting purposes to be one hundred percent accurate, an 'almost there' status is sufficient for the SME entrepreneur to understand the financial impact of their day-to-day management. Most bookkeepers can prepare an SME's financials to around eighty percent accuracy of the level required for income tax or statutory accounting purposes.

- **Consistency**

Consistency refers to the treatment of like transactions and the timing of these transactions. Similar transactions need to be recorded and processed in the same manner from one month to the next. This allows the totals and balances to be relied upon and interpreted accurately.

Ultimately, you must be consistent with the method upon which your financial statements are prepared, whether you choose the Cash Basis or Accrual Basis of accounting. To switch between the two will distort the information presented. Because most accounting databases cater to both processes, it is only a matter of entering the transactions per the date they occur.

You also need to be consistent with the timing of recording your transactions and preparing your financial statements. This will ensure that when you report regularly, you are including all applicable transactions.

Once you have determined the three core financial statements have been prepared consistently, then you can rely upon any comparisons you make from one reporting period, month or year, to the next. This is invaluable for any subsequent decisions you make.

When the three criteria of 'timely, accuracy and consistency' are applied to transactions and statements, your Finance Engine will provide you with a comprehensive financial summary of business activity that you can make decisions upon with confidence.

No Time like the Present: The When

AS WE DISCERNED *which* SME's should prepare the three financial statements, *when* they should be prepared is also dependent upon the size of the SME.

- ***Micro SME***—should prepare the cash flow statement on a quarterly or monthly basis at a minimum.
- ***Small SME***—should prepare the Profit & Loss Statement and Cash Flow Statement on a monthly basis at a minimum.
- ***Medium SME***—should prepare the three core financial statements on a monthly basis regarding a hard close. They should also conduct a review of the interim statements on a mid-month, fortnightly or weekly basis, referred to as a soft close.

A hard close refers to the books being fully reconciled and will ensure that the three financial statements are accurate. A soft close refers to the books that are not necessarily fully reconciled, but the transactions have been processed up to the current date and are in a condition that will show the financial position and flow of transactions for the month.

A soft close enables the business owner to capture any deficiencies or business activity that is falling short of expectations or is moving in an undesirable direction within the hard close reporting period. This provides opportunity to implement changes or strategies to improve the hard close results.

Remember the 'timely' criteria; it makes sense to prepare reports as often as possible to ensure discrepancies can be identified and appropriate solutions implemented right away. Monthly is the most common reporting period.

Delays are frequently expensive and your ultimate objective as an entrepreneur is to conserve cash and allocate your SME's resources in areas that are most conducive to business growth and sustainability. It is better to know sooner than later when activity goes haywire.

Remember, accurate figures do not lie.

We have looked at the what, who, why, how and when of preparing the three core financial statements and the functions they serve in your SME's Finance Engine.

We discussed the importance of appointing a bookkeeper to compile your accounting records, allowing you time to comprehensively review your financial statements and analyse the information they report. This helps improve your decision-making so you can become a more effective small business manager.

We also covered the three sizes of SMEs and the level of investment they should apply in preparing the three core financial statements. To be effective, the financial statements need to meet the criteria of timely, accuracy and consistency. You must also prepare them using one of two methods: Cash Basis of accounting or Accrual Basis of accounting. The financial statements should be prepared and reviewed regularly.

We can now discuss the three core financial statements in detail. In Part Two, we will outline the importance and purpose of each statement, the elements they report upon, the relationship between the elements, the relationship between the three financial statements, and how you can preserve the health of each statement and your SME. We will revisit Sam's Dilemma and detail his journey as he discovers his Finance Engine.

Part 2

The Three Platforms to Financial Freedom

CHAPTER 1

Without Profits, What's the Point

The Measure of Your Business

Case Study—Sam's Profit and Loss

The bookkeeper needed three days to get their financials up to-date and in a condition ready for review. Sam didn't understand why it took so long since Beth always stayed on top of it, but he was content to let Debra take as long as she wished since they agreed to a lump sum payment. His only concern was securing the bank loan in time to pay Jake by the 30th of June.

The bookkeeper insisted they meet to discuss the financial statements she compiled. All three of them sat about the small table they utilised for such important discussions. Debra had her laptop set up with their accounting database at the ready, and she provided each of them with a hard copy of the three financial statements she had prepared. At the least, she was organised.

"Shall we start with the Profit & Loss?" the bookkeeper asked confidently.

"We can skip it. I've been looking at it from time to time and know where we stand."

She smiled. "I understand you've been using the simple format to calculate net profit. I've actually prepared the Profit & Loss Statement using a format that will provide you with three levels of profit. It can be instrumental in understanding where your net profit comes from and, in turn, can help with cash management."

Sam's lips twitched. She knew he was concerned about his cash flow. Funny, he didn't recall mentioning it. "Okay then, take it away."

There is nothing more exciting for the budding entrepreneur than their first sale. It is a milestone reached after days, weeks, months and sometimes even years, and it casts you in a successful glow. With a proficient and results-driven marketing engine, the sales roll in and the bank balance grows—or does it? There is a common misconception that profits are cash and should show up on the bank statement. However, this is not necessarily the case because not all business expenditure is captured by the Profit & Loss Statement. The core purpose of the P&L is to calculate profits.

A business cannot be sustained by only selling your gift in the form of services and/or product and making sales. While you may have brought in $100,000 in sales in a certain month, you must still pay for the goods and services you acquired or utilised to generate these sales. For your SME to be viable, you need to have money left over after you have settled these expenses. To be profitable, you need to generate a higher value in sales than you have incurred in expenditures and derive positive earnings.

It is just as important to focus on your profit as it is to focus on the quantity of sales, which is where the Profit & Loss Statement comes in. By preparing a P&L, you can verify if your business activity is profitable or if you incurred a loss. Remember, a sale is not a viable sale if it costs more to generate than you earned from it.

Characteristics of the Profit & Loss Statement

The Profit & Loss Statement is the first of the three core financial statements and is the one that the small business owner is most familiar with. Why? Most likely because it is the financial statement that government taxation agencies rely on to calculate the income tax payable on the earnings you have made.

However, government taxation bodies should not be the business owner's core motivation for preparing the Profit & Loss Statement. The entrepreneur has a vested interest in preparing this statement to ensure they are profiting from their investment of time and other resources. When you understand the value of the statement, you can not only use it to report your SME's earnings but also to identify opportunities to minimise your costs and maximise your revenue and profitability.

As it states, the Profit & Loss Statement calculates the Net Profit or Loss, or earnings resulting from the business operations by deducting all expenses incurred from revenue earned. It can also be referred to as the Income Statement or The Statement of Earnings.

It is not feasible to wait the full life of an entity to determine whether or not its business activity is profitable, so it is broken down into periods referred to as accounting periods or reporting periods. The Net Profit or Loss, or earnings of the business, will capture revenue and expense transactions over this defined period; this time is usually represented by a month, a quarter or a year.

For this reason the Profit & Loss Statement is described as a flow statement, or a period statement, because it provides information from one point in time to another. This flow is like a river where the start and end of the river represents the life of the entity and sections of the river from one point to another would represent the reporting period assigned.

I also view the Profit & Loss Statement like blood in the human body. No human body can survive without it, so we must ensure the flow is consistent and ample to sustain life. Its continual flow throughout our body enables the use of our arms and legs. We can say much the same about the profits of the SME. They need to be consistent, ample and of a sufficient level to finance the SME's operational activity and maintain the infrastructure of the business. Profits need to be ongoing.

Good business practice requires the Profit & Loss Statement to be prepared and reviewed monthly to ensure any decreases in revenue or increases in expenses are identified in a timely fashion and that the integrity of the enterprise's Net Profit is maintained. Remember, as long as preparation of the statement adheres to the three criteria for effectiveness—timely, accuracy and consistency—then you can rely upon the statement with confidence.

Previously we mentioned it is the business owner's role to analyse. To analyse the Profit & Loss Statement effectively, the business owner needs to understand each of the P&L's elements, their nature and the relationship they have with one another. They should understand the concepts of Gross Profit, Operating Profit and Net Profit and how they differ so the statement can assess the effectiveness of sales achieved on net profit and manage it accordingly.

Though analysis of the Profit & Loss Statement should be conducted monthly, during periods of crisis or uncertainty, it may be necessary to do so on an interim basis during the month for immediate action. The analysis process itself should identify discrepancies and highlights to understand the profits or losses particular business activities generate. Should any problems be identified, you can then act upon them promptly and strive to preserve future month's net profits.

Cash vs Accrual Accounting

You recall that financial statements are prepared on either the Cash Basis of accounting or Accrual Basis of accounting.

When the Profit & Loss Statement is prepared on a cash accounting basis, it will represent the consolidated value of transactions for each element on the date that cash was transferred to pay for an expense or received for products sold or services rendered. Revenue would represent the total value of cash received from customers during the reporting period. Expense values show the amount of cash paid regarding that expense. On a cash Profit & Loss Statement, the Net Profit line will represent the net cash received as a result of regular trading activity.

Please note that even a cash Profit & Loss Statement does not communicate your SME's full cash situation. A cash P&L will only report the cash profits your business earns from normal operations and not the net cash of *all* cash receipts and *all* cash payments.

When the Profit & Loss Statement is prepared on an accrual accounting basis, it will represent the consolidated value of transactions for each element based upon the date the revenue was earned and expense was incurred. If an invoice is raised for a customer or by a supplier, it will represent the date revenue was earned or an expense was incurred irrespective of whether cash was received or paid on the same date. As with the Cash Basis, the profit reported on the accrual Profit

& Loss Statement does not report on the SME's full cash position.

The profit calculated will be different under each accounting basis. Neither is more accurate than the other; it is presenting the same information in a different form. This is because of the difference in the timing transactions are recognised.

It is important to understand the method chosen to prepare the Profit & Loss Statement, and you need to apply it consistently from one month to the next. You can then determine the actual value represented in the statement, which will instill confidence in the information reported and will enable you to decipher the information presented accurately, making the most out of comparisons from one month or year to the next.

The Format of the Profit & Loss Statement

There are several forms that the Profit & Loss Statement can take. In its simplest form, the P&L Statement can calculate a net profit by deducting all expenses from total revenue, which is more than sufficient to calculate your net profit for a reporting period. However, the standard approach is to calculate the three levels of profit that contribute to the overall net profit.

The simplest format of the Profit & Loss Statement rests on the following calculation.

Net Profit equals Revenue less Expenses

Net Profit = Revenue - Expenses

The Profit & Loss Statement in the simplest format is presented as follows:

Business Name

Profit & Loss Statement
April 202X

		Amount
Revenue	$	100,000
Less Expenses	$	80,000
Net Profit / (Loss)	**$**	**20,000**

This format will provide information on the revenue earned during the month and the total value of expenses incurred to generate that revenue, resulting in a net profit of $20,000. Because there is no further information provided, the reader is unaware of whether this level of revenue and profit is comparable to other months or if it is a positive result.

The Profit & Loss Statement presented in the most common format appears as follows:

Business Name
Profit & Loss Statement
April 202X

	Month to Date	% of Sales	Year to Date	% of Sales
Revenue	$ 99,000	100.00%	$ 1,195,000	100.00%
Less Cost of Sales	$ 60,000	60.61%	$ 725,000	60.67%
Gross Profit	**$ 39,000**	**39.39%**	**$ 470,000**	**39.33%**
Less Overhead Expenses	$ 20,000	20.20%	$ 200,000	16.74%
Operating Profit	**$ 19,000**	**19.19%**	**$ 270,000**	**22.59%**
Other Revenue & Expenses	$ 1,000	1.01%	$ 5,000	0.42%
Net Profit / (Loss)	**$ 20,000**	**20.20%**	**$ 275,000**	**23.01%**

From even a cursory glance, you can see the depth of information this format provides. By presenting the month's Profit & Loss Statement in a format that provides three levels of profit, year-to-date values and a percentage assessment of where the line items are regarding revenue, the reader gets much more information to analyse if the net profit achieved is acceptable.

The standard format of the Profit & Loss Statement usually has five columns: accounts, amount and percentage of sales for the Month (MTD), and amount and percentage of sales for the year-to-date (YTD).

The accounts column is on the left-hand side of the report and represents revenues and expenses. The elements of Revenue, Cost of Sales, Overhead Expenses and Other Revenue & Expenses can be broken out into more detailed accounts. The account names reflect the expense types, like rent and revenue, or domestic sales and overseas sales. These detailed accounts discern the nature of the revenue or expense and the categories group and consolidate like accounts together.

The amount column reports figures for each of the revenue and expense accounts and represents the consolidated sum of the transactional activity for the chosen period. The month column will display the value for the month, and the year to-date column will represent the total value for the financial year to the end of the month reported.

The percentage of sales columns represents the expense or revenue as a percentage of total revenue. This enables the reader to determine if a particular account is within or outside of the expected range for a particular period.

The standard format of the Profit & Loss Statement will provide more information than the simplest format. You can take the standard format further to maximise the value of the P&L by customising the statement specifically to your business activity. This will enable you, the business owner, to process the information provided swiftly and in context without the need to assume or guess. We will look further at customising the Profit & Loss Statement in chapter three, *The Blood of Your Entity*.

The standard format of the P&L will sufficiently calculate the net profit of your business' activity for a defined period. It provides three levels of profit: Gross Profit, Operating Profit and Net Profit. In chapter two, we look at the elements of the Profit & Loss Statement regarding overall net profit.

Case Study—Sam's Profitability

The bookkeeper generated a Profit & Loss Statement for April and displayed it on her laptop. She directed Sam and his wife's attention to their report pack and asked them to locate the Profit & Loss Statement in her preferred format and compare it with the one on the screen.

Sam found no need to look at the format on her laptop in detail. He gave it a cursory glance, determining there were no remarkable differences. However, he noted the figures differed somewhat from what he'd expected based on his previous reports. For now, he kept his mouth shut and turned his attention to the Profit & Loss Statement in her format.

Debra became more animated as she discussed the differences between the two statements, enjoying her work. The revenue at the top of the report and the net profit at the bottom of the two reports were the same, but she had grouped the expenses into two different types. Before Sam could ask why, she directed them to the three levels of profit presented on the statement. She insisted they were vital to understanding their business and they would discuss each of them further.

For now, she wanted the couple to understand the figures displayed were accrual figures, not cash amounts. They were the summation of customer invoices raised and supplier invoices dated and processed during April. Sam thought it seemed straightforward, but continued to listen.

Below is the format Sam had been using when generating the report.

Sam's Landscaping & Design

Profit & Loss Statement

April 202X

		Month to Date	% of Sales		Year to Date	% of YTD Sales
Revenue	$	211,703	100.00%	$	1,773,056	99.50%
Asset Sales	$	-	0.00%	$	8,880	0.50%
Total Revenue	**$**	**211,703**	**100.00%**	**$**	**1,781,936**	**100.00%**
Expenses						
Accounting Fees	$	1,925	0.91%	$	28,565	1.60%
Advertising	$	2,097	0.99%	$	24,970	1.40%
ASIC License Fees	$	380	0.18%	$	380	0.02%
Bank Fees & Charges	$	205	0.10%	$	2,050	0.12%
Branded Stationary	$	240	0.11%	$	10,480	0.59%
Dues & Subscriptions	$	834	0.39%	$	1,086	0.06%
Electricity	$	461	0.22%	$	5,186	0.29%
Electronic Communication Exp	$	99	0.05%	$	909	0.05%
Entertainment Expenses	$	664	0.31%	$	7,524	0.42%
Gas	$	288	0.14%	$	2,634	0.15%
Insurance	$	704	0.33%	$	7,042	0.40%
Interest Expense	$	897	0.42%	$	8,966	0.50%
Income Tax Expense	$	-	0.00%	$	12,458	0.70%
Labour Expenses	$	45,524	21.50%	$	412,040	23.12%
Material Purchases	$	97,754	46.18%	$	832,100	46.70%
Motor Vehicle Expenses	$	6,097	2.88%	$	32,856	1.84%
Office Supplies	$	1,234	0.58%	$	7,299	0.41%
Plant & Equipment Expenses	$	1,088	0.51%	$	22,767	1.28%
Postage	$	123	0.06%	$	1,235	0.07%
Rent & Outgoings	$	4,433	2.09%	$	44,330	2.49%
Telephone	$	1,247	0.59%	$	11,706	0.66%
Water	$	276	0.13%	$	1,405	0.08%
Total Expenses	**$**	**166,571**	**78.68%**	**$**	**1,477,988**	**82.94%**
Net Profit / (Loss)	**$**	**45,132**	**21.32%**	**$**	**303,948**	**17.06%**

Below is the format the bookkeeper prefers to use.

Sam's Landscaping & Design

Profit & Loss Statement

April 202X

	Month to Date	% of Sales	Year to Date	% of YTD Sales
Revenue				
Hard Landscaping	$ 112,871	53.32%	$ 894,295	50.44%
Soft Landscaping	$ 42,032	19.85%	$ 361,160	20.37%
Builders Contract Revenue	$ 56,800	26.83%	$ 517,600	29.19%
Total Revenue	**$ 211,703**	**100.00%**	**$ 1,773,056**	**100.00%**
Cost of Sales				
Material Purchases	$ 97,754	46.18%	$ 832,100	46.93%
Labour Expenses	$ 45,524	21.50%	$ 412,040	23.24%
Plant & Equipment Expenses	$ 1,088	0.51%	$ 22,767	1.28%
Motor Vehicle Expenses	$ 6,097	2.88%	$ 32,856	1.85%
Total Cost of Sales	**$ 150,464**	**71.07%**	**$ 1,299,763**	**73.31%**
Gross Profit	**$ 61,239**	**28.93%**	**$ 473,292**	**26.69%**
Overhead Expenses				
Accounting Fees	$ 1,925	0.91%	$ 28,565	1.61%
Advertising	$ 2,097	0.99%	$ 24,970	1.41%
ASIC License Fees	$ 380	0.18%	$ 380	0.02%
Bank Fees & Charges	$ 205	0.10%	$ 2,050	0.12%
Branded Stationary	$ 240	0.11%	$ 10,480	0.59%
Dues & Subscriptions	$ 834	0.39%	$ 1,086	0.06%
Electricity	$ 461	0.22%	$ 5,186	0.29%
Electronic Communication Exp	$ 99	0.05%	$ 909	0.05%
Entertainment Expenses	$ 664	0.31%	$ 7,524	0.42%
Gas	$ 288	0.14%	$ 2,634	0.15%
Insurance	$ 704	0.33%	$ 7,042	0.40%
Interest Expense	$ 897	0.42%	$ 8,966	0.51%
Office Supplies	$ 1,234	0.58%	$ 7,299	0.41%
Postage	$ 123	0.06%	$ 1,235	0.07%
Rent & Outgoings	$ 4,433	2.09%	$ 44,330	2.50%
Telephone	$ 1,247	0.59%	$ 11,706	0.66%
Water	$ 276	0.13%	$ 1,405	0.08%
Total Overhead Expenses	**$ 16,107**	**7.61%**	**$ 165,767**	**9.35%**
Operating Profit	**$ 45,132**	**21.32%**	**$ 307,526**	**17.34%**
Other Revenue & Expenses				
Asset Sales	$ -	0.00%	$ 8,880.00	0.50%
Income Tax Expense	$ -	0.00%	($ 12,458)	(0.70%)
Total Other Revenue & Expenses	**$ -**	**0.00%**	**($ 3,578)**	**(0.20%)**
Net Profit / (Loss)	**$ 45,132**	**21.32%**	**$ 303,948**	**17.14%**

Sam spent some time studying the differences. The Profit & Loss Statement with the three levels of profit seemed like overkill. He noticed that the net profit percentage for the year was different on both formats whilst the total amount of net profit was the same.

Remembering Paul's promise that this process was worth the effort, Sam kept this observation to himself. He glanced at his wife and her smile told him she was thinking the same thing.

"Shall I continue?" Debra asked when Sam caught her eye.

He nodded.

Now that you understand the purpose of the Profit & Loss Statement, we can look at the individual elements in more detail. We have touched on the three levels of profit and in the next chapter titled "The Ingredients of Profitability," we will look at these profit levels in more detail, outlining how they are calculated and what they mean to your business. We will also address the Revenue and Expense elements and why they are represented as they are in the standard Profit & Loss Statement format.

CHAPTER 2

The Ingredients of Profitability

Elements of the P&L

THERE IS MORE to the Profit & Loss Statement and its elements than just reporting your SME's Net Earnings or Net Profit for the month or year. When you classify your revenue and expenses and present them on the Profit & Loss Statement in the standard format, it will calculate three levels of profit. Each level of profit communicates different information to the reader, enabling you to make informed decisions to maximise profitability.

The three levels of profit calculations are Gross Profit, Operating Profit and Net Profit. The results and relationships are unique to your business. Understanding their natures and relationships to revenue will put you in a better position to make effective decisions when considering increasing revenue by price or by volume and provide you with an understanding of how many sales units you need to sell to make an overall Net Profit. The calculation of the three profit levels become exceedingly important when assessing your desired level of Net Profit and the strategies you need to implement.

The base upon which we calculate these three profit levels rests upon the classification of the Revenue and Expense accounts. Revenue is split into Operating Revenue and Other Revenue. Expenses are split into Cost of Sales, Overhead Expenses and Other Expenses. These revenue and expense categories are then used to calculate the three levels of profit: Gross Profit, Operating Profit and Net Profit.

The key elements of the Profit & Loss Statement are:

- Revenue;
- Cost of Sales;
- Gross Profit;
- Overhead Expenses;
- Operating Profit;
- Other Revenue & Expenses;
- Net Profit.

We will discuss each element in detail. To enhance our discussion, I suggest you generate your entity's fully reconciled Profit & Loss Statement for a completed reporting period and refer to it as we reference each element. As your Profit & Loss Statement outlines the result of your SME's business' activity it will naturally be more meaningful and assist you in grasping the concepts. I have provided examples referencing the case study, *Sam's Landscaping & Design*.

Some of these elements are straight-forward, while others are more in depth. Understanding the nature and purpose of each of these elements is vital for you to interpret the three levels of profit calculated on your Profit & Loss Statement effectively and to make decisions that improve your profitability rather than compromise it.

Operating Revenue

Where would businesses be without revenue?

Maintaining consistent and reliable revenue streams is vital to keeping our SME operating. When reading a Profit & Loss Statement, the business owner needs to understand how it is calculated and what it is reporting upon. Most entrepreneurs will be across what revenue is: sales. The discussion below will focus on revenue's place on the P&L and its importance regarding the other statement elements.

Operating Revenue is reported at the top of the Profit & Loss Statement. It is usually listed as Revenue but can also be called Sales or Income. Your P&L might display a list of the revenues earned within your business or be a single line representing your total sales.

Operating Revenue is defined as follows:

> ***Revenues*** *are the earnings a business receives from selling goods and or providing services to customers. It is also sometimes referred to as income or sales. It is recurring in nature and represents the sales of the core solution your entity offers to the market.*

Under accrual accounting, Operating Revenue is recognised when an invoice is raised representing the earning of income or the receipt of cash, whichever event occurs first. Under cash accounting, this occurs when cash is received from selling a product and/or providing a service irrespective of the associated invoice's date.

An example of a revenue item is the fees earned from services rendered or the sales of products. Regarding our case study, revenue is earned from landscape projects which are a combination of services and a finished product. It is important that Operating Revenue is distinct from Other Revenue which is reported later in the Profit & Loss Statement. For now, the primary difference is Operating Revenue is recurring—it is the sum of all transactions that occur on a day-to-day basis.

Operating Revenue serves as the anchor of the Profit & Loss Statement. Its value is used as a base to measure all other elements on the Profit & Loss Statement. This relationship is usually reported as a percentage. The percentage of revenue is used to assess whether an element is within or outside the expected or desired percentage range. We will discuss this relationship for each element.

Regarding Revenue, the percentage will always be one hundred percent.

Cost of Sales

Unfortunately, to make money you need to spend money. The Cost of Sales is important because it represents an expenditure that must be spent to bring in revenue. While most entrepreneurs will understand which of these expenditures are critical in providing their service, they are not always reported separately on the Profit & Loss Statement. It is important to separate them from other expenditures to calculate the margin you earn on sales. Below, we will discuss where Cost of Sales fits on the P&L and its unique relationship with revenue.

Cost of Sales is a category of expense used in the calculation of Gross Profit. It represents funds going out of the business and is reported under the Operating Revenue line.

Before we look at Cost of Sales further, let's look at the definition of Expenses.

> ***Expenses** are costs incurred in earning of revenue from which no future benefit beyond a period of twelve months is expected.*

The benefits of such costs are consumed within a year. Expenses can be classified into Cost of Sales, Overhead Expenses or Other Expenses.

Examples of expenses would be telephone costs incurred in day-to-day business or materials purchased to manufacture a product you sell to earn revenue.

In the simplest form a business's profit can be calculated:

Revenue less Expenses equals Profit

Revenue – Expenses = Profit

The calculation above is an accurate way to determine the profit you make from your business activity. However, if you only calculate your business activities' overall profit, you will miss out on the benefits of calculating the three profits levels: Gross Profit, Operating Profit and Net Profit.

Each profit level provides important information to use when deciding how to increase your revenue line, which increases your ultimate Net Profit. The decisions you make based on elements above the Gross Profit line will be different to decisions you make from below it to generate a similar impact on Net Profit.

To enable the calculation of these three profit levels, you need to classify your list of expenses into categories based upon their nature. This nature is defined by how they relate to the operating revenue your business activity earns. The categories that expenses can be grouped into are Cost of Sales, Overhead Expenses and Other Expenses. For now, the distinction between these categories is that Cost of Sales can be linked directly against Operating Revenue while the other two cannot.

Let's look at the definition of Cost of Sales.

***Cost of Sales** is a category of expenses that are also referred to as cost of goods sold in a business that sells products. Costs of sales* *are all costs that can be directly linked to getting goods and or services into a condition and location for sale. These costs do not provide a future benefit, but an immediate benefit to the business and are consumed within a twelve-month period.*

An example of Cost of Sales is the cost of labour used to provide a service for a service-based business or the cost of manufacturing the product you sell for a product-based business. In a project-based business, like our case study, Cost of Sales can be a combination of both labour and product.

As a general rule, as operating revenue increases, so does cost of sales proportionally. While the absolute value of cost of sales will increase as absolute value of operating revenue increases, the percentage of the Cost of Sales to Operating Revenue will stay relatively the same.

The benefit of identifying expenses as Cost of Sales is that you are isolating and grouping expenses that possess a similar nature. They have a direct relationship with Revenue in that they must be purchased in order to generate revenue. Having identified the costs directly associated with revenue, you can calculate a level of profit that will rise and fall in line with operating revenue.

This level of profit is called the Gross Profit.

Gross Profit

Gross Profit is the first of the three profit calculations on the Profit & Loss Statement. It represents the margin your SME makes on your revenue.

Gross Profit should always be positive. When it is negative, we refer to it as a Gross Loss. If you are generating a gross loss, you need to make radical changes to bring it into a positive state. As long as you are incurring a gross loss, you will never make an overall net profit no matter how many units you sell. For this reason, it is imperative to understand the Gross Profit measurement.

Gross Profit is defined as follows:

> ***Gross Profit*** *is what is left from Operating Revenue after Cost of Sales has been taken into account. It is also sometimes referred to as the Contribution Margin.*

Gross Profit can also be explained as the difference between Revenue and Cost of Sales, and is calculated as follows:

Gross Profit equals Revenue less Cost of Sales

Gross Profit = Revenue – Cost of Sales

Gross Profit is reported on the Profit & Loss Statement in two forms: an absolute value and a percentage of revenue. While the term Gross Profit refers to the absolute value of gross profit, the percentage of revenue is called the Gross Profit Margin.

The Gross Profit and Gross Profit Margin reflect the summation of what your SME earns on sales. The margin on each unit of sale multiplied by the volume sold will equate to the total Gross Profit earned. The Gross Profit Margin represents the absolute gross profit as a percentage of revenue. Total Gross Profit Margin will be similar to the margin percentage calculated on one unit of sale.

It is important to understand the difference between the absolute Gross Profit and Gross Profit Margin and their relationship with Revenue. When you increase the volume of your sales resulting in higher revenue, you will also increase the absolute value of your gross profit. If your goal is to increase the absolute Gross Profit, then increasing sales volume will achieve this.

However, if your objective is to increase your Gross Profit Margin, you will not achieve this by increasing your sales volume. As long as the same level of unit costs are incurred to enable each unit of sale, the Gross Profit Margin will remain the same percentage of revenue, at every volume level of sales.

An increase in your Gross Profit Margin is an increase in the gross profit's percentage of revenue. You can increase your Gross Profit Margin in one of three ways—by increasing the sales value of your product or service, decreasing your cost of sales by unit, or both.

When your SME is incurring a Gross Loss, you will need to implement strategies that will convert the gap between revenue and cost of sales to generate a positive margin.

By increasing the price of your sales unit relative to the cost of its inputs, you will generate more revenue for the same cost. By decreasing the cost of inputs relative to revenue—for example, using fewer inputs or negotiating better prices—you will increase the margin you make on each sale. If you both increase your sales prices and decrease the total cost of inputs per sales unit, you will also increase the difference between Revenue and Cost of Sales and increase your Gross Profit Margin.

Understanding any increase in volume will only change the absolute value of Gross Profit and not the Gross Profit Margin, is a useful tool in managing your SME's overall Net Profit.

Case Study—Sam's Gross Profit Dilemma

Satisfied Sam and Beth were accepting of the more detailed statement, the bookkeeper meticulously explained every element on the Profit & Loss Statement. She described how each element related to their business activity, how each had been calculated and the relationship they each had with revenue. Starting with revenue, Sam realised this meeting was going to take a while.

Sam always split his P&L revenue into three revenue streams—hard landscaping, soft landscaping and builder's contract revenue. This enabled him to determine which revenue stream contributed most to his SME's total revenue for the month and the year. As of year-to-date, fifty percent of his total revenue had been earned from hard landscaping, twenty percent from soft landscaping, and twenty-nine percent from the two residential construction companies he contracted to. The bookkeeper highlighted that total revenue reported at one hundred percent.

From Sam's perspective, the more detailed Profit & Loss Statement showed no major difference regarding revenue to the statement he had been using. The only exception was the revenue from the digger they sold earlier in the year. It was no longer included.

Sam remembered the digger sale was not classified as Operating Revenue, but Other Revenue. Debra, seeming to have read his mind, explained it would be displayed later in the statement and redirected Sam to the next element.

Sam's Landscaping & Design

Profit & Loss Statement

April 202X

		Month to Date	% of Sales		Year to Date	% of YTD Sales
Revenue						
Hard Landscaping	$	112,871	53.32%	$	894,295	50.44%
Soft Landscaping	$	42,032	19.85%	$	361,160	20.37%
Builders Contract Revenue	$	56,800	26.83%	$	517,600	29.19%
Total Revenue	**$**	**211,703**	**100.00%**	**$**	**1,773,056**	**100.00%**
Cost of Sales						
Material Purchases	$	97,754	46.18%	$	832,100	46.93%
Labour Expenses	$	45,524	21.50%	$	412,040	23.24%
Plant & Equipment Expenses	$	1,088	0.51%	$	22,767	1.28%
Motor Vehicle Expenses	$	6,097	2.88%	$	32,856	1.85%
Total Cost of Sales	**$**	**150,464**	**71.07%**	**$**	**1,299,763**	**73.31%**
Gross Profit	**$**	**61,239**	**28.93%**	**$**	**473,292**	**26.69%**

Cost of Sales was the first category of expense reported and sat under the total revenue line. The cost of sales for Sam's Landscaping & Design included material purchases, labour expenses, plant and equipment expenses and motor vehicle expenses. Each of these expenses were incurred to get the landscapes ready and/or completed, and had a direct link with revenue.

Sam inspected the expenses the bookkeeper grouped under Cost of Sales. He had to agree he had no choice but to sustain each of these costs to execute and complete each job. Timber, pavers, labour to install, the hire of equipment and the cost of getting to and from the sites. Materials were reported at forty-seven percent of revenue for the year, and labour was at twenty-three percent. The equipment he hired and the motor vehicle expenses were minimal at less than four percent combined.

Upon reflection, the high material cost surprised him. He noticed the percentages in April for each of the cost of sale expenses were essentially the same for the year so far. Total cost of sales for April were at seventy-one percent and for the year so far at seventy-three percent.

The bookkeeper then provided a Profit & Loss Statement for the past four months, which included the revenue and cost of sales for each month.

Sam's Landscaping & Design

Profit & Loss Statement

February to April 202X

	JAN	% Sales	FEB	% Sales	MAR	% Sales	APR	% Sales
Revenue								
Hard Landscaping	$ 47,487	71.33%	$ 105,526	51.79%	$ 116,084	51.64%	$ 112,871	53.32%
Soft Landscaping	$ 19,089	28.67%	$ 42,240	20.73%	$ 45,490	20.24%	$ 42,032	19.85%
Builders Contract Revenue	$ -	0.00%	$ 56,000	27.48%	$ 63,200	28.12%	$ 56,800	26.83%
Total Revenue	**$ 66,576**	**100.00%**	**$ 203,766**	**100.00%**	**$ 224,774**	**100.00%**	**$ 211,703**	**100.00%**
Cost of Sales								
Material Purchases	$ 25,741	38.66%	$ 99,197	48.68%	$ 115,962	51.59%	$ 97,754	46.18%
Labour Expenses	$ 22,537	33.85%	$ 39,622	19.44%	$ 43,531	19.37%	$ 45,524	21.50%
Plant & Equipment Expenses	$ 2,107	3.17%	$ 2,704	1.33%	$ 2,713	1.21%	$ 1,088	0.51%
Motor Vehicle Expenses	$ 2,203	3.31%	$ 2,464	1.21%	$ 3,089	1.37%	$ 6,097	2.88%
Total Cost of Sales	**$ 52,588**	**78.99%**	**$ 143,987**	**70.66%**	**$ 165,294**	**73.54%**	**$ 150,464**	**71.07%**
Gross Profit	**$ 13,987**	**21.01%**	**$ 59,779**	**29.34%**	**$ 59,480**	**26.46%**	**$ 61,239**	**28.93%**

Sam looked at the percentage of sales for the Total Cost of Sales for the months of February through April. It hovered around seventy to seventy-four percent, despite there being a twenty thousand absolute value difference between the lowest revenue month, February and the highest revenue month, March. April's revenue and cost of sales fell between both these two months in absolute value and as a percentage of operating revenue. As revenue increased, so did the absolute amount of cost of sales. As revenue decreased, cost of sales also decreased.

Regarding the percentage change, Debra explained that while revenue between February and March had increased by ten percent, the cost of sales percentage of revenue had only increased by three percent. This was due to the mix of materials, equipment and labour used rather than the fluctuation in revenue.

Sam studied the report whilst the bookkeeper explained how it showed their SME's operating activity was consistently earning a positive margin on revenue earned. Sam was pleased when she said that this was a good sign.

It still didn't explain why there wasn't any cash in his bank account.

Debra then brought Sam's attention to the gross profit line on the Profit & Loss Statement that reported the month of April and year-to-date results. The gross profit for April was $61,000, and the gross profit margin was almost twenty-nine percent of revenue. The gross margin for the year to-date was almost the same at twenty-seven percent. Sam thought about this as he reviewed the P&L, recalling the bookkeeper's reference to the gross profit being similar to the margin on each job.

"Wait a minute. The gross profit margin isn't right," Sam announced suddenly. "When I quote, I always use a margin of forty percent. The gross profit margin should be closer to that, not twenty-seven!"

"Actually, Sam, you mentioned you apply a lower margin to Thrifty Investments and Benefit Homes because they guarantee you volume sales and each job is relatively the same in area and

costs incurred. There are also instances when you applied discounts to residential jobs to ensure you got them and Beth mentioned you only charged your mates at cost," Debra reminded him diplomatically. "These will have a significant effect on the gross profit margin."

"But a thirteen percent drop?" Sam huffed.

"We investigated this, Sam," Beth said. "We discounted almost every residential job we did in April. It was also the month we did Craig's job, which took longer than we'd expected." Beth didn't hide her resentment about his best mate's demands.

"And the boys worked weekends, which means higher labour costs," Sam concluded.

"All of which will push the gross profit margin down," Debra confirmed. "It is quite probable that you're not including all the costs in your quotes that have been captured at Cost of Sales in the statement. This will also affect the gross profit calculation."

Sam looked at the report. He never included motor vehicle expenses in his quotes, and he knew that occasionally equipment hired on the go was missed. However, looking at plant & equipment and motor vehicle expenses percentage of revenue, this made only a minor impact on gross profit and didn't explain the thirteen percent deficiency.

"Are you sure this is right?" Sam waved the hard copy report.

"Yes. Beth and I fully reconciled every element on all three statements. If not one hundred percent accurate, I am confident we have captured every transaction, and it is exceedingly close," the bookkeeper assured.

With further thought, Sam realised Debra was alluding to his invoices missing additional materials purchased during the job and the impact of unaccounted overtime. Both costs he was incurring without passing them on to the customer.

Sam shook his head. All this time he'd been confident he was earning forty percent on every job. Referring back to the quarterly report, it showed the gross profit margin was consistently between twenty-six and twenty-nine percent. With the year-to-date gross profit margin at twenty-seven percent, it meant this had been happening for some time. He wondered when it started to slip.

"We've been taking on more jobs to pick up the slack in paying our bills," Sam justified.

"Increasing your sale volume will only increase what you have to pay out in cost of sales. If you want to improve your cash flow, you can do so by increasing your margin. Meaning, increasing the price you are charging customers, decreasing the cost of your inputs or both," the bookkeeper explained.

"You can manage your work schedule so you only do one discounted job each month and only do mate's projects in quiet periods. I would even put into place a policy to have all additional costs approved by the customer before implementation. Then review all costs incurred on a job at the time of invoicing, rather than invoicing the quote at the start of the job. It will make a big difference very quickly."

"And we can learn all of this just by having a gross profit line on the Profit & Loss Statement?" Sam asked in disbelief.

"Sure can. It's important to review the gross profit margin each month to ensure it's not only meeting your expectations but also to ensure that it's high enough to meet your net profit objectives. The beauty of it being on the Profit & Loss Statement is your overall margin on your sales is calculated for you and you only need to run the report to check it. However, when you do, just be certain all transactions have been entered and have been..."

"Fully reconciled," Sam completed.

Debra nodded. "Shall I continue?"

"Please."

What Sam learned about the profitability of his business unearthed him. How much more was happening he didn't know about? Beth flashed him a heartening expression and a sense of calm came over him. Maybe Paul was right. They may need to take these reports more seriously.

The Gross Profit on the Profit & Loss Statement is the first of the three profit levels and is the key to managing your SME's profitability and operating cash. Understanding the difference between the absolute Gross Profit and the Gross Profit Margin becomes more significant when we take into account Overhead Expenses. It can mean the difference in turning an overall Net Loss into a Net Profit, or making a Net Profit that meets your expectations.

Overhead Expenses

Money is not only spent on Cost of Sales to generate Revenue. You also need to allocate your hard-earned money on maintaining the infrastructure of your business model and on goods and services that can enhance the delivery of your service or product. These are expenses that are not linked to a specific unit of sales, but still occur regularly and are just as important in the provision of your core solution as Cost of Sales or input costs are. These expenses are classified as Overhead Expenses.

Overhead Expenses represent the cost of maintaining the business model of the SME.

Below we will look at how Overhead Expenses are reported on the Profit & Loss Statement and how their relationship with Revenue differs to the Cost of Sales. We will also discuss the relationship Overhead Expenses have with the absolute Gross Profit and how this is the key to making Net Profits.

Previously we mentioned that expenses can be classified into Cost of Sales, Overhead Expenses and Other Expenses. Overhead Expenses are reported next on the Profit & Loss Statement underneath the Gross Profit line.

Overhead Expenses differ from Cost of Sales in their relationship with Operating Revenue. While Cost of Sales expenses are linked on a unit-by-unit basis with Revenue,

Overhead Expenses are not. Overhead Expenses are set by other variables not directly associated with the goods and or services you are selling, but are required to produce them. Unlike Cost of Sales, the variables that drive Overhead Expenses are not directly linked to revenue like cost of sales expenses are.

Overhead Expenses also differentiate from Other Expenses in that they are recurring and the result of day-to-day business activity. They will reoccur daily, weekly, monthly or even yearly, whereas Other Expenses are one-off expenditures and uncommon to your normal trading.

> ***Overhead Expenses*** *are expenses not directly related to the production of goods and/or services, but are still incurred while providing the productive activity of the business. The benefits overhead expenses provide are consumed within twelve months.*

Two examples of overhead expense are advertising expenses incurred for a promotion to sell more product and/or services to increase operating revenue, or rent for the premises your business operates from. In both cases, it is expenditure not required to prepare your product or service for sale directly, but is required to drive the normal functioning of your business.

As a rule, overhead expenses have a tendency to stay consistent regarding their absolute value from one reporting period to the next. There may occasionally be a significant rise due to an annual charge in one reporting period, however, as expenses are usually charged regularly, the spread is generally even across a year.

There is no guaranteed relationship between Overhead Expenses and Revenue as there is for Cost of Sales. Overhead expenses can rise and fall independently as revenue increases and decreases. The resulting percentage of revenue could rise as revenue rises, or rise when revenue falls, or fall when revenue rises, or fall when revenue falls. This lack of relationship is highlighted when Overhead Expenses differ significantly from one reporting period to the next.

When these expenses are broken into instalments or monthly charges and are incurred regularly, the total absolute overhead expense will be relatively the same from one reporting period to the next. When this occurs, we can see a relationship with revenue forming where the overhead expense percentage of revenue will fall as revenue rises or rise as revenue levels fall.

The relationship of steady overhead expenses will continue to rise as revenue falls, or fall as revenue levels rise until a significant change is made to the infrastructure of your SME's business model. When you alter the structure of your business model, you affect the running expenses of that structure. As a result, your SME's absolute overhead expenses from one reporting period to the next can increase or decrease significantly. In this instance, the percentage of Overhead Expenses to Revenue will undergo a step change. When a step change occurs, as overhead expenses increase, the percentage of revenue will also increase, and as overhead expenses decrease, the percentage of revenue will also decrease.

Since the relationship of Overhead Expenses to Revenue is relatively unpredictable, it is more beneficial to track the absolute amount of Overhead Expenses from one reporting period to the next and measure it against your absolute Gross Profit. Remember, that overhead expenses reflect the cost of maintaining your business model, so it is important to understand the likely annual absolute amount. With your annual overhead expenditure in mind, you will know the annual level of absolute gross profit required to cover your overhead expenditure.

The ultimate objective is to ensure your SME achieves Overhead Coverage. Overhead Coverage occurs when the absolute gross profit is equal to or greater than the absolute value of overhead expenses. When Overhead Coverage is achieved, the next level of profit, Operating Profit, can be determined.

Operating Profit

Operating Profit is the next item reported on the Profit & Loss Statement. It takes into account expenses classified as Cost of Sales and Overhead Expenses; Other Expenses are excluded. Like Gross Profit, Operating Profit reflects the management of your normal business activity and its financial impact. Until this profit point, you can influence the profit made when making decisions that impact incoming revenue, cost of sales and overhead expenses.

> ***Operating Profit*** *is profit generated from normal trading activities. Any revenue or expenses that are unusual or considered outside of normal trading are not taken into account when calculating operating profit.*

Operating Profit is calculated on the Profit & Loss Statement as follows:

Operating Profit equals Gross Profit less Overhead Expenses

Operating Profit = Gross Profit – Overhead Expenses

Operating Profit is distinct from Net Profit. The importance of calculating Operating Profit rests upon the premise that it's within the scope of your entity's normal business activity and under your management. This profit level will capture the net financial impact of your decisions.

The Operating Profit section on the P&L captures decisions resulting in increased or decreased revenue, decisions affecting the costs of your core solution's inputs, and changes made to your business model structure and maintenance. By understanding the financial impact of your decisions, you can influence your SME's operating profit.

The Operating Profit calculation is the cascading effect of revenue as it falls to Gross Profit and Operating Profit. The revenue remaining after cost of sales expenses are deducted is reported on the Gross Profit line. Revenue left after deducting cost of sales and overheads will be reported on the line for Operating Profit. By making informed and deliberate decisions that influence revenue, cost of sales and overhead expenses, you can manage your SME's Operating Profit.

You may embark on an advertising campaign that successfully generates increased revenue. You may purchase improved quality input materials that cost more and increase your cost of sales. Or you may move locations and subsequently alter your rent and associated building costs. These decisions have a financial impact and will be reflected in the Operating Profit line of your Profit & Loss Statement.

If you are not happy with your current operating profit, you can influence it by making strategic decisions that impact the elements above this line and raise the operating profit made. Operating profit reflects your skills as a financial manager, as all Profit & Loss Statement elements to this point are influenced by decisions you make in the management of your business activity.

To achieve an operating profit, your business activity would need to generate a gross profit level that covers your overhead expenses. When the absolute value of gross profit falls short and is less than the absolute value of overhead expenditure, an operating loss will result. To ensure operating profitability, you need to establish a level of absolute gross profit that exceeds your overhead expenses. The margin earned on your sales needs to cover the running costs of your business model.

The actions you would need to take if you are incurring an operating loss are determined by the absolute gross profit. If gross profit is negative and reporting a gross loss, you will need to make radical changes to the price of your service or product, cost of sales, or both to move your gross profit margin into a positive status.

Remember, increasing the volume of sales will only result in an increase in absolute value of gross profit and not the gross profit margin. In a situation of incurring a gross loss, an increase in the volume of sales will only increase the absolute value of the gross loss.

If your gross profit is positive, yet you are incurring an operating loss, you are not achieving overhead expenses coverage. You can remedy this in one of three ways. You can put measures in place to reduce the cost of maintaining your business model structure. You could implement strategies to increase the volume of sales and generate more revenue and the absolute value of gross profit. Or, you can improve your gross profit margin by increasing revenue, decreasing cost of sales, or both.

The importance of reporting a Gross Profit distinct from Operating Profit increases in significance when you understand how your decisions can influence these two profit elements. If your Profit & Loss Statement does not distinguish between Gross Profit & Operating Profit, you could make decisions in an attempt to improve your profitability that instead compromise your chances of achieving this, or even make the situation worse.

The same poignancy results in the third profit distinction of Net Profit. While Gross Profit is the result from the sale of your solution, Operating Profit is the result of your business model providing that solution. Operating Profit is distinct from Net Profit because it is the net financial result of normal recurring business activity whereas Net Profit is not.

Case Study—Sam's Operating Profit Dilemma

The bookkeeper spent considerable time discussing their business model and how the running costs were captured under Overhead Expenses on the Profit & Loss Statement. She explained they were different to Cost of Sales in that they didn't rise and fall in line with operating revenue. Sam's overhead expenses were relatively even from month to month in absolute value with occasional impact from significant annual costs. Irrespective of what revenue was earned, overhead expenses were incurred anyway.

Debra directed their attention to the overhead expenses reported below the gross profit line on the Profit & Loss Statement. She said the percentage of revenue of their overhead expenses were relatively light at less than ten percent for the year so far, a good sign their business model was maximising the return on each dollar invested and focused upon generating revenue.

For the first ten months of the financial year, they had spent almost $166,000 in overhead expenses. Projected over a full twelve-month period, they would need approximately $200,000 to cover their annual overhead costs. This was the cost of maintaining their current business model.

"Considering you're generating revenue of around two million annually, your overhead costs are far from excessive."

Sam was pleased to hear that. When he looked at the statement, he noted that after rent, accounting fees were his largest annual expense.

As though reading his mind, Debra said, "The exception is the accounting fees. I can help with that and make sure they are less in the future."

Sam pursed his lips; she was a saleswoman. He suspected she was seeking further work out of this exercise.

Sam's Landscaping & Design

Profit & Loss Statement

April 202X

		Month to Date	% of Sales		Year to Date	% of YTD Sales
Total Revenue	**$**	**211,703**	**100.00%**	**$**	**1,773,056**	**100.00%**
Total Cost of Sales	**$**	**150,464**	**71.07%**	**$**	**1,299,763**	**73.31%**
Gross Profit	**$**	**61,239**	**28.93%**	**$**	**473,292**	**26.69%**
Overhead Expenses						
Accounting Fees	$	1,925	0.91%	$	28,565	1.61%
Advertising	$	2,097	0.99%	$	24,970	1.41%
ASIC License Fees	$	380	0.18%	$	380	0.02%
Bank Fees & Charges	$	205	0.10%	$	2,050	0.12%
Branded Stationary	$	240	0.11%	$	10,480	0.59%
Dues & Subscriptions	$	834	0.39%	$	1,086	0.06%
Electricity	$	461	0.22%	$	5,186	0.29%
Electronic Communication Exp	$	99	0.05%	$	909	0.05%
Entertainment Expenses	$	664	0.31%	$	7,524	0.42%
Gas	$	288	0.14%	$	2,634	0.15%
Insurance	$	704	0.33%	$	7,042	0.40%
Interest Expense	$	897	0.42%	$	8,966	0.51%
Office Supplies	$	1,234	0.58%	$	7,299	0.41%
Postage	$	123	0.06%	$	1,235	0.07%
Rent & Outgoings	$	4,433	2.09%	$	44,330	2.50%
Telephone	$	1,247	0.59%	$	11,706	0.66%
Water	$	276	0.13%	$	1,405	0.08%
Total Overhead Expenses	**$**	**16,107**	**7.61%**	**$**	**165,767**	**9.35%**
Operating Profit	**$**	**45,132**	**21.32%**	**$**	**307,526**	**17.34%**

Sam continued studying the Overhead Expenses listed on his Profit & Loss Statement whilst Debra continued discussing the relationship between overhead expenses and revenue.

"The relationship of overheads with revenue is different to cost of sales, which you can see when we look at the P&L for the months of February to April." She directed Sam's attention to a report showing Overhead Expenses from January to April.

Sam's Landscaping & Design

Profit & Loss Statement
January to April 202X

	JAN	% Sales	FEB	% Sales	MAR	% Sales	APR	% Sales
Total Revenue	**$ 66,576**	**100.00%**	**$ 203,766**	**100.00%**	**$ 224,774**	**100.00%**	**$ 211,703**	**100.00%**
Total Cost of Sales	**$ 52,588**	**78.99%**	**$ 143,987**	**70.66%**	**$ 165,294**	**73.54%**	**$ 150,464**	**71.07%**
Gross Profit	**$ 13,987**	**21.01%**	**$ 59,779**	**29.34%**	**$ 59,480**	**26.46%**	**$ 61,239**	**28.93%**
Overhead Expenses								
Accounting Fees	$ -	0.00%	$ 1,925	0.94%	$ 20,865	9.28%	$ 1,925	0.91%
Advertising	$ 2,097	3.15%	$ 2,097	1.03%	$ 2,097	0.93%	$ 2,097	0.99%
ASIC License Fees	$ -	0.00%	$ -	0.00%	$ -	0.00%	$ 380	0.18%
Bank Fees & Charges	$ 205	0.31%	$ 205	0.10%	$ 205	0.09%	$ 205	0.10%
Branded Stationary	$ 1,095	1.64%	$ -	0.00%	$ 1,600	0.71%	$ 240	0.11%
Dues & Subscriptions	$ -	0.00%	$ -	0.00%	$ -	0.00%	$ 834	0.39%
Electricity	$ 285	0.43%	$ 525	0.26%	$ 505	0.22%	$ 461	0.22%
Electronic Communication Exp	$ 90	0.14%	$ 90	0.04%	$ 90	0.04%	$ 99	0.05%
Entertainment Expenses	$ 200	0.30%	$ 500	0.25%	$ 500	0.22%	$ 664	0.31%
Gas	$ -	0.00%	$ 543	0.27%	$ -	0.00%	$ 288	0.14%
Insurance	$ 704	1.06%	$ 704	0.35%	$ 704	0.31%	$ 704	0.33%
Interest Expense	$ 897	1.35%	$ 897	0.44%	$ 897	0.40%	$ 897	0.42%
Office Supplies	$ 522	0.78%	$ 1,200	0.59%	$ 794	0.35%	$ 1,234	0.58%
Postage	$ 123	0.19%	$ 123	0.06%	$ 124	0.06%	$ 123	0.06%
Rent & Outgoings	$ 4,433	6.66%	$ 4,433	2.18%	$ 4,433	1.97%	$ 4,433	2.09%
Telephone	$ 548	0.82%	$ 1,259	0.62%	$ 1,386	0.62%	$ 1,247	0.59%
Water	$ -	0.00%	$ 277	0.14%	$ -	0.00%	$ 276	0.13%
Total Overhead Expenses	**$ 11,199**	**16.82%**	**$ 14,778**	**7.25%**	**$ 34,201**	**15.22%**	**$ 16,107**	**7.61%**
Operating Profit	**$ 2,788**	**4.19%**	**$ 45,001**	**22.08%**	**$ 25,279**	**11.25%**	**$ 45,132**	**21.32%**

Sam inspected the report and discovered that whilst in January, February and April Total Overhead Expenses were around $11,000 to $15,000 and $16,000, for March they were almost $35,000. The peak was caused by those pesky accounting fees, a required but regrettable expense related to last year's tax return. Many other lines were the same from month to month, while other increases, like office supplies, fluctuated independently of revenue.

Sam saw the percentage of revenue for January's Overhead Expenses shot up to nearly seventeen percent. Though similar in March, there was no such annual expense in January, and the absolute amount was only $11,000. The jump was because of the fall in revenue. Sam had to agree there was no apparent proportional relationship with revenue.

"It therefore makes more sense," Debra continued, "to measure your overheads against the absolute gross profit level. As long as the absolute gross profit is greater than your total overhead expenses, you will generate an operating profit. You've more than covered your overheads each month this year. Although, you will see in January that gross profit only just covered your overheads. This is due to the large drop in operating revenue of around $150,000."

"No surprises there. January has always been a dead month because of summer holidays. The building industry breaks the day before Christmas and doesn't return until the third week of January at least," Sam rationalised. "We also encourage the boys to take leave around the same time so it doesn't disrupt the work schedule during the year."

"It's important to preserve the absolute gross profit on months like that to ensure overhead coverage."

"That means no margin discounts and no cost-only jobs during those months, right?"

"Right."

Debra pointed to the operating profit line on the Profit & Loss Statement. For April, it was twenty-one percent of revenue and for the year thus far it was over seventeen percent. She explained that while considered a good level, if changes were made to influence the gross profit margin in an upward direction and closer to Sam's preferred forty percent, the operating profit would also improve.

"That's because the decision to improve the gross profit margin of your current business model will not impact overhead expenses," she explained.

"So, if I make sure we earn forty percent on each job and the gross profit margin reached forty percent, what would the operating profit be?"

"An increase in gross profit, or decrease for that matter, with no change to your business model, will fall directly to the operating profit line. If you increase the gross profit margin by thirteen percent and made no other changes that impact your overhead expenses, you could earn an operating profit of thirty percent."

Sam's excitement grew. He wondered how an increase in his operating profit would affect his cash levels.

"Would that improve my cash situation?" Sam asked tentatively. He didn't want the bookkeeper to know how desperate he was to rectify his cash balance.

"Of course. As operating profit increases, so too will the cash you generate from normal operations. However, the overall impact on your cash balance depends on how quickly you're growing. We'll look at your cash more closely when we discuss the Balance Sheet and the Cash Flow Statement."

"Okay, so, what's the significance of calculating net profit if operating profit is the profit level we can manage?"

"You need to include all expenses to calculate bottom line net profit. For your business to be sustainable you need to continue making overall net profits, not just operating profits. It's also the profit level tax agencies use to determine how much you need to pay to the government in income tax. Sometimes net profits can be considerably different to operating profit and is dependent upon the other revenue and expense items."

Other Revenue & Expenses

Customary business trading is often affected by events external to your business and beyond the boundary of what you can control. The financial impact of these external events can sometimes be so significant, they consume profits you otherwise would have made. These need to be captured by the Profit & Loss Statement to calculate the overall profit of your business. However, value can be gained from separating the revenue and expense items from your SME's operating profit, so you understand the true results of your decisions and the environment you operate within.

Revenue or expense transactions that occur outside of the normal business activity of the entity are described as extraordinary. Such revenue and expenses are reported on the Profit & Loss Statement on the 'Other Revenue & Expense' line, enabling the distinction between Operating Profit and Net Profit.

> ***Other Revenue & Expenses*** *capture revenue and expense items that are unavoidable and outside of the normal operations of your business activity. This line is sometimes referred to as Other Income.*

Other Revenue and Expenses are reported on the Profit & Loss Statement below the Operating Profit. Accounts listed under this classification are reported as a positive figure for revenue and a negative figure for expenses, calculating a net value. When the net figure is positive, it is added to the operating profit. When the net value is negative, it is deducted from operating profit.

Sometimes a business will earn revenue from means other than selling their core services and or products. They may sell a machine that is no longer required to manufacture product sold in the normal course of business, or interest may be received for a loan the business made to a third party which is revenue that is not a consistent part of their usual business trading. Securities and shares that were invested in may be sold to gain access to their value in cash. Even revenue received from a government grant may need to be included on the Profit & Loss Statement. In such cases, when it is not a normal operating item, it is classified under Other Revenue.

Likewise, if a business incurs expenditure outside the normal scope of their trading, it is also reported at the Other Revenue & Expense line. This may include income tax expenses or loss on the sale of an asset below its original purchase price. These could be recovery costs associated with the impact of a natural disaster, such as a tsunami or bush fires, or the additional cost of terminating employees for downsizing.

By reporting these extraordinary expenses on this line of the Profit & Loss Statement, you will preserve the profit you earn from normal trading and report Operating Profit. When Other Revenue and Expenses are separated from Cost of Sales and Overhead Expenses, you can calculate the third line of profit—Net Profit.

Net Profit

Net Profits, or a healthy bottom line, is the objective of any commercial entity. As long as your SME is making net profits most months and annually, you are making a net margin on the sale of your services and/or product. However, it is a misconception that net profits equate to cash. The Profit & Loss Statement is only one of the three core financial statements the SME should prepare. Therefore, it reports on only one-third of the business activity that influences your cash balance.

The ultimate aim of the Profit & Loss Statement is to calculate the net profits your SME makes each reporting period. Net Profit represents the final earnings after taking into account all the business' revenue and expenditure from all the business' activity for a reporting period. It is defined:

> ***Net Profit*** *is the profit generated from all business activities, normal and extraordinary. Net profit is also commonly referred to as the bottom line. It is the difference between all revenue and all expenses.*

Net Profit is presented on the P&L after the Other Revenue & Expenses line and is most often referred to as the "bottom line" because it is the last line on the statement. It is displayed as an absolute value and also as a percentage of revenue.

Net Profit can be calculated by deducting from Revenue the Cost of Sales and Overheads and adding the net Other Revenue and Expenses incurred during a reporting period. Unlike Operating Profit, it encompasses all extraordinary items. Taking into account all the elements on the Profit & Loss Statement, it can be calculated using one of the following three calculations. No matter which calculation is used, the net profit calculated will be the same.

Net Profit equals Revenue less Cost of Sales less Overheads plus Other Revenue & Expenses

Net Profit = Revenue – Cost of Sales – Overhead Expenses + Other Revenue & Expenses

OR

Net Profit equals Gross Profit less Overhead Expenses plus Other Revenue & Expenses

Net Profit = Gross Profit – Overhead Expenses + Other Revenue & Expense

OR

Net Profit equals Operating Profit plus Other Revenue and Expenses

Net Profit = Operating Profit + Other Revenue and Expenses

A positive net profit is the earnings objective of conducting your core business activity. Over time, accumulated net profits will add to the equity you hold in your business. Should net losses occur, these will reduce the equity you hold in your business. Net Profits/Losses are reported on the Balance Sheet where the Equity you hold is reported. This will be discussed further in chapter five, *The Recipe of Stability*.

Case Study—Sam's Net Profit

The bookkeeper next reviewed the bottom of the Profit & Loss Statement, where Other Revenue and Expenses were listed under the operating profit line and before net profit.

Sam's Landscaping & Design

Profit & Loss Statement

April 202X

		Month to Date	% of Sales		Year to Date		% of YTD Sales
Revenue							
Hard Landscaping	$	112,871	53.32%	$	894,295		50.44%
Soft Landscaping	$	42,032	19.85%	$	361,160		20.37%
Builders Contract Revenue	$	56,800	26.83%	$	517,600		29.19%
Total Revenue	**$**	**211,703**	**100.00%**	**$**	**1,773,056**		**100.00%**
Cost of Sales							
Material Purchases	$	97,754	46.18%	$	832,100		46.93%
Labour Expenses	$	45,524	21.50%	$	412,040		23.24%
Plant & Equipment Expenses	$	1,088	0.51%	$	22,767		1.28%
Motor Vehicle Expenses	$	6,097	2.88%	$	32,856		1.85%
Total Cost of Sales	**$**	**150,464**	**71.07%**	**$**	**1,299,763**		**73.31%**
Gross Profit	**$**	**61,239**	**28.93%**	**$**	**473,292**		**26.69%**
Overhead Expenses							
Accounting Fees	$	1,925	0.91%	$	28,565		1.61%
Advertising	$	2,097	0.99%	$	24,970		1.41%
ASIC License Fees	$	380	0.18%	$	380		0.02%
Bank Fees & Charges	$	205	0.10%	$	2,050		0.12%
Branded Stationary	$	240	0.11%	$	10,480		0.59%
Dues & Subscriptions	$	834	0.39%	$	1,086		0.06%
Electricity	$	461	0.22%	$	5,186		0.29%
Electronic Communication Exp	$	99	0.05%	$	909		0.05%
Entertainment Expenses	$	664	0.31%	$	7,524		0.42%
Gas	$	288	0.14%	$	2,634		0.15%
Insurance	$	704	0.33%	$	7,042		0.40%
Interest Expense	$	897	0.42%	$	8,966		0.51%
Office Supplies	$	1,234	0.58%	$	7,299		0.41%
Postage	$	123	0.06%	$	1,235		0.07%
Rent & Outgoings	$	4,433	2.09%	$	44,330		2.50%
Telephone	$	1,247	0.59%	$	11,706		0.66%
Water	$	276	0.13%	$	1,405		0.08%
Total Overhead Expenses	**$**	**16,107**	**7.61%**	**$**	**165,767**		**9.35%**
Operating Profit	**$**	**45,132**	**21.32%**	**$**	**307,526**		**17.34%**
Other Revenue & Expenses							
Asset Sales	$	-	0.00%	$	8,880.00		0.50%
Income Tax Expense	$	-	0.00%	($	12,458)	(	0.70%)
Total Other Revenue & Expenses	**$**	**-**	**0.00%**	**($**	**3,578)**	**(**	**0.20%)**
Net Profit / (Loss)	**$**	**45,132**	**21.32%**	**$**	**303,948**		**17.14%**

Sam's Landscaping and Design didn't report any extraordinary revenue or expenses in April that would be classified as Other Revenue and Expenses. He did, however, sell a digger for just under $9,000 earlier that financial year. This sale was listed under the Other Revenue and Expense category.

Previously, Sam included it in the total revenue calculation at the top of the statement. He supposed that by reporting it at Other Revenue and Expenses, it allowed the percentage of revenue calculation for each element to relate only to his operating revenue from normal trading. The sale of the digger would have distorted that calculation and marred the relationship of other elements to Operating Revenue.

Sam took a deeper look at the statement. He noticed the income tax he paid on last year's return was also reported here.

"Shouldn't income tax be before operating profit? It's a normal part of trading," Sam asked.

"Yes, it's an annual charge and occurs from usual trading, however reporting it under Overhead Expenses will distort your operating profit. Wouldn't you like to know what your operating profit is before tax?"

Sam nodded.

"The amount reported at income tax expense also relates to last year's earnings. By removing it from the operating profit calculation, you can make an estimate of the tax you are likely to pay on normal operations ongoing and before having to pay it. While your tax accountant will make adjustments to your books when preparing your tax return, you can estimate from month to month what you can expect to pay and not get the same surprise you got last year."

"That would be nice."

"The company tax rate in Australia is presently twenty-six percent, so tax payable for this financial year so far will be near $80,000. Any instalments you've already made will be deducted from this. We'll talk about this more when we look at the Balance Sheet."

Debra ran through the structure of the Profit & Loss Statement once more, summarising the impact of the classification of the revenue and expense elements and how they were used to calculate the three levels of profit.

Sam conceded this Profit & Loss Statement format with the three profit lines was significantly more informative than the one they used previously. He now knew more about how his business profit was calculated and how his decisions affected it, having gone through this analysis with Debra.

However, Sam was still at a loss about his cash situation.

"I don't understand. If I'm making hundreds of thousands in profits why do I never have any cash in my bank account?" Sam finally asked, hoping to leave the desperation out of his voice.

Debra smiled. "This is the most common question asked of me."

She explained how the Profit & Loss Statement affected cash.

Profit and Cash are not Equal

The purpose of the Profit & Loss Statement is to calculate profit. Net profits will contribute to your cash balance via cash deposits and cash payments associated with revenue and expense items, however rarely will net profits equal the net cash deposited for the same reporting period. There are two reasons the net profit calculated may not equal the cash deposited in your bank account for the reporting period.

First, cash accounting or accrual accounting.

You recall the Profit & Loss Statement is prepared on one of two methods. The Cash Basis of accounting, or the Accrual Basis of accounting. As soon as you raise customer invoices to be paid at a later date, your revenue line on the Profit & Loss Statement will report the total of customer invoices in the reporting period. It will include both customer invoices that have been paid and those that have not been paid. The total revenue will represent an accrual calculation of revenue.

The same situation applies to expenses. If you are processing supplier invoices and paying them at a later date, each of your expense elements will be captured by the Profit & Loss Statement at the date of the invoice. Some of these supplier invoices may have been paid during the same reporting period, reducing your cash balance, and some may not have been paid. As a result, the total of all expenses will not be equal to the total of expenses actually paid.

If the P&L has been prepared on the Cash Basis of accounting, the Revenue and Expense elements will report the cash received or cash paid regarding that element. Cash received and paid for revenue and expenses will increase or decrease your cash balance, however they still may not capture all the cash deposits and cash payments made.

This brings us to the second reason the reported Net Profit does not necessarily equal cash deposits. The Profit & Loss Statement is only one of the three core financial statements that the SME should prepare and only represents one-third of your business' financial landscape. Therefore, it only reports on one-third of your cash movements and does not illustrate the complete picture from month to month.

Cash deposits and cash payments are also elements of the Balance Sheet. We will discuss cash movements in more detail as we progress through the chapters on the Balance Sheet and the Cash Flow Statement. For now, it is important to understand that the Profit & Loss Statement calculates your SME's net profit and only represents one-third of the activity driving cash in and out of your entity.

You should now have a thorough understanding of the three lines of profit reported on the Profit & Loss Statement: Gross

Profit, Operating Profit and Net Profit. Each profit level is calculated by classifying your expenditure as either Cost of Sales, Overhead Expenses or Other Expenses.

With this knowledge in hand, you are better equipped to understand how your decisions impact your profitability and how to maximise those profits. You can make more financially effective decisions and produce the best possible returns on your investment of time and money.

The core solution your business provides should be the focus of your business activity. The Net Profit generated from that business activity is a by-product, the result. There will be times when decisions you need to make for qualitative benefits have financial implications that impact your net profit negatively. Knowing the impact of the Profit & Loss Statement elements will allow you to plan and develop expectations that would otherwise be a surprise and could result in expensive lessons learned.

CHAPTER 3

The Blood of Your Entity

Let's Keep the Blood of Your Business Pumping!

SO, WHAT DOES a healthy Profit & Loss Statement look like?

This is a million-dollar question. Many factors will influence what a healthy P&L Statement should look like, and they are as individual as your business.

The first driver, and the one you have full control over, is the structure and layout of your business model. A business model is the infrastructure of your business and how you produce and deliver your core service and or product. Your business model will play a large part in the financial support you require and the flow of your transactions through your SME, affecting your financial statements.

We have already alluded to Overhead Expenses being the maintenance costs of running your business model. Whether you operate your business from home, out of a rented premise, or an owned premise, there is a financial impact. Financial impacts will differ depending on if you are a service-based entity or are offering a product. If you require heavy investment in machinery and equipment, there will be a financial impact. When you employ staff or use casual or contract labour, there are different statutory requirements you must meet and they will have a financial impact.

The business model you design to produce and deliver your offering will dictate the effects upon your financial statements. Regarding the Profit & Loss Statement, there will be Revenue, Cost of Sales, Overhead Expenses and Other Revenue and Expenses specific to the business model you have chosen.

There are other factors that will affect your SME's Profit & Loss Statement. There are factors external to your business and usually outside of your management in the sense that they impose requirements upon you. Different industries have various governing and statutory requirements, and different markets will require investment in various technologies. Licensing requirements are imposed to set standards, and governments will impose minimum expectations regarding labour management and safety requirements. Each of these external drivers impose conditions and requirements that will have a financial impact on your business model.

To understand levels of profitability specific to your industry, you can consult government bodies that collate these statistics for your region. In Australia, the Bureau of Statistics is a good source of such information. In the United States, the U.S. Census Bureau or the Bureau of Labor Statistics is a source of industry specific trends and statistics. In Canada, the national office of Statistics Canada is the government body, and in the United Kingdom, the Office for National Statistics gathers this information.

I have outlined below a generic set of variables that characterise a healthy Profit & Loss Statement. Review these variables while taking into consideration the impact of external requirements imposed upon you in your industry and by governments in your region. Generally, the more stringent the statutory requirements, the lower the profit levels specific to you and your industry.

Healthy Status of the Profit & Loss Statement	
Element	**Health Status**
Revenue	As long as revenue is relatively consistent from month to month and has an upward trend, this line reviewed in isolation would be considered healthy. For start-ups the level of revenue may not generate an operating profit at first, however it should show an increasing trend and heading towards a profitable level. For established businesses, a healthy revenue level should generate operating profits comfortably.
Gross Profit	40% of revenue or higher.
Operating Profit	20% of revenue or higher. The heavier your business model structure, the greater the impact on operating profit. For low-cost business models, operating profit should be greater than 20%. For high-cost business models, operating profit may only be around 10%.
Net Profit	10% of revenue or higher. Some highly competitive industries with low value products may be significantly lower than 10%. In situations where extreme external conditions have had a severe impact, a positive result would be unlikely and considered favourable.

Premise of the Profit & Loss Statement

We looked at what constitutes a healthy Profit & Loss Statement. The analysis of your P&L may fall short in some metrics provided and you may wish to implement actions to improve the lines reported.

While the Revenue line is a distinct result of your marketing engine and the activities it makes up, you can affect changes to the Profit & Loss Statement by making small decisions regarding the mix and source of the expenditure listed or much larger decisions regarding how your business operates. The one premise upon which the P&L rests is your ability to quote and the sale price you apply to your service and or product whilst minimising the cost of inputs and overhead costs of your business model.

The Revenue line of your Profit & Loss Statement reflects the summation of the selling price of products and/or services sold during the reporting period. The Cost of Sales represents the cost of inputs that can be tracked unit by unit against each hourly rate charged for service and the selling price on a unit of product. Overhead Expenses will represent the cost of the infrastructure of the business model. Therefore, the pricing/quoting of your product or service should be at a level that covers all of your business costs on a unit by unit basis.

When quoting or pricing products, we often remember the direct input costs but often omit the expenses that have no direct link to the product or service we sell. It is important to remember when quoting or pricing our product to include a specific amount to cover your business structure costs, that is your Overhead Expenses.

Whilst we said that the relationship of overhead expenditure to revenue was unpredictable and could fluctuate up and down according to many variables, it is easiest to include a set percentage of revenue to cover your overhead costs when you quote. To ensure Overhead Coverage you would then manage the volume of sales to ensure absolute Gross Profit is high enough.

As a general rule, you should apply ten percent when determining your price based upon your business costs. A higher percentage often results in overloading the costs per one unit of sale.

If the analysis of your Profit & Loss Statement against the generic metrics has produced discrepancies you wish to correct, you can do so by revisiting the pricing and quoting of your service or product.

The analysis above will ensure you cover all business costs subject to selling a set number of units of service and or product. It is important to take into account two considerations:

1. Not to overburden your unit price with overhead costs.
2. Be aware of the price dictated by the market.

Quoting and pricing effectively is only achieved when you do not overburden the unit price with your business model's maintenance costs. You need to be conservative in the allocation of your overhead expense coverage and establish a reasonable expectation regarding a level of volume that is achievable and will cover your overhead expenses. This is a balancing act and one that is specifically driven by the environment within which you run your business, your business model and the industry or industries.

The second consideration is the price dictated by the market in which you operate. If you operate within larger economies with many players, you may find that to secure a share of the market and divert customer loyalty to your product, you need to price your product in line with the market. To command a higher price than that dictated by the market will require adding value to your product. In such a case where you must assume the market price, you can influence your margin by implementing strategies that decrease your input costs to increase your margin.

Once you understand how your quotes and prices relate to and impact the elements on the Profit & Loss Statement, you can make informed decisions and take action to improve it. Note that it takes time to implement changes and any assessment of your P&L after such a change is implemented should ensure that a full month is impacted by this change before analysing the results. Gradually you will move towards the targets you have established and improve your profitability.

Case Study—The Health of Sam's Profit & Loss Statement

The bookkeeper explained whether Sam's Profit & Loss Statement would be considered healthy. They discussed Sam's expectations for his business and what he would like to achieve. They then set targets he wanted to reach for each element.

The table below summarises the results of their discussion.

Sam's Landscaping & Design – Profit & Loss Statement Targets		
Element	**Target**	**Actual Result**
Revenue	Monthly Average: $250,000 Annual Average: $3 million	Monthly Average: $177,000 Annual Average: $2 million
Gross Profit	40% of revenue	Under at 26.69%
Operating Profit	30% of revenue.	Under at 17.34%
Net Profit	20% of revenue or higher.	Under at 17.14%

The three of them went over strategies Sam could implement to raise the actual result to meet his new targets. Most of them could be implemented immediately and would convert into rapidly improved results.

Below is the list of strategies they developed.

- *Ensure a forty percent mark-up when quoting (the forty percent includes ten percent to contribute to overhead coverage);*
- *Estimate ten percent additional labour to cover overtime when quoting;*
- *Implement an additional works form for customer approval and update original quote;*
- *Invoice from the last full quote provided to customer;*
- *Invoice all completed jobs at the end of the week;*
- *Only discount one job per month;*
- *Only conduct projects for mates in slow months with no public holidays;*
- *Schedule labour so employees with expertise work on residential jobs (better cost coverage and more interesting work for higher-skilled labour) and;*
- *Review Profit & Loss Statement monthly and measure against set targets.*

Sam reviewed the list with Beth and they were pleased the list of changes were manageable and could be implemented both relatively easily and quickly.

Benefits of Customising the Profit & Loss

The impact of your business model and industry requirements will be specific to your business. The financial impact will also be specific to your business. It makes sense to generate a Profit & Loss Statement specific to your business and your decision-making needs.

There is considerable value gained by customising your Profit & Loss Statement to your business activity as you can tailor it to the areas of your business you wish to concentrate upon.

The Standard Profit & Loss Statement will generally report on the month to-date (MTD) and year to-date (YTD) absolute sum of transaction values for the reporting period and provide a percentage of revenue analysis on each line. This enables the reader to make a comparison between the month to-date period's results against those achieved for the financial year to-date. At a quick glance, the reader can determine if the month's results are in line with that achieved year to-date. Discrepancies should be highlighted and further investigation conducted to gain an understanding of why they occurred.

You can take a step further in tailoring your Profit & Loss Statement by grouping your Revenue and Expense accounts with like transactions, providing totals and percentage of revenue status for each group. Cost of Sales and Overhead Expenses can be grouped into further categories meaningful to your business and help when analysing your monthly P&L Statement.

By grouping like accounts together, you can generate a summarised version of the Profit & Loss Statement, which may provide you with more meaning than a list of only revenue streams and expense accounts. This will result in more effective decision-making and management of your business activities, toward improving gross profit and operating profit.

The best format for your business is the one you will use. It should provide you with profit-and-loss information in a manner that enhances your decision-making ability by presenting the information in a concise and informative manner.

This format will change from one business to the next and will require some forethought.

Case Study—Customising Sam's Profit & Loss Statement

Besides reporting the three lines of profit, the bookkeeper explained that Sam could also benefit from making further customisation to the Profit & Loss Statement format to provide more clarity to the report.

Sam's Landscaping & Design report already provided more details about the revenue streams activity than Sam had seen before. Debra suggested he could further detail his Cost of Sales by having individual accounts for types of materials and motor vehicle costs. She also suggested grouping his overhead expenses together by type.

In the report package Debra provided, there were two other Profit & Loss Statement formats. One was a summarised version, and the other was a fully detailed version.

She explained they could use the summarised version in the future to assess the actual results against the targets Sam set. If he required further information on a particular account, he could first look at the detailed P&L for an explanation before going any further.

The summarised Profit & Loss Statement for Sam's Landscaping & Design had a single line for revenue and grouped the overhead expenses into categories of marketing expenses, office expenses, building expenses, professional expenses and finance expenses.

She presented it as follows.

Sam's Landscaping & Design
Profit & Loss Statement
April 202X

	Month to Date	% of Sales	Year to Date	% of YTD Sales
Revenue	$ 211,703	100.00%	$ 1,773,056	100.00%
Total Revenue	**$ 211,703**	**100.00%**	**$ 1,773,056**	**100.00%**
Cost of Sales				
Material Purchases	$ 97,754	46.18%	$ 832,100	46.93%
Labour Expenses	$ 45,524	21.50%	$ 412,040	23.24%
Plant & Equipment Expenses	$ 1,088	0.51%	$ 22,767	1.28%
Motor Vehicle Expenses	$ 6,097	2.88%	$ 32,856	1.85%
Total Cost of Sales	**$ 150,464**	**71.07%**	**$ 1,299,763**	**73.31%**
Gross Profit	**$ 61,239**	**28.93%**	**$ 473,292**	**26.69%**
Overhead Expenses				
Marketing Expenses	$ 3,001	1.42%	$ 42,974	2.42%
Office Expenses	$ 2,704	1.28%	$ 21,149	1.19%
Building Expenses	$ 5,458	2.58%	$ 53,555	3.02%
Professional Expenses	$ 3,139	1.48%	$ 30,031	1.69%
Finance Expenses	$ 1,806	0.85%	$ 18,058	1.02%
Total Overhead Expenses	**$ 16,107**	**7.61%**	**$ 165,767**	**9.35%**
Operating Profit	**$ 45,132**	**21.32%**	**$ 307,526**	**17.34%**
Other Revenue & Expenses				
Asset Sales	$ -	0.00%	$ 8,880	0.50%
Income Tax Expense	$ -	0.00%	($ 12,458)	(0.70%)
Total Other Revenue & Expenses	**$ -**	**0.00%**	**($ 3,578)**	**(0.20%)**
Net Profit / (Loss)	**$ 45,132**	**21.32%**	**$ 303,948**	**17.14%**

The more detailed Profit & Loss Statement is on the following page.

Sam's Landscaping & Design

Profit & Loss Statement
April 202X

	Month to Date	% of Sales	Year to Date	% of YTD Sales
Revenue				
Hard Landscaping	$ 112,871	53.32%	$ 894,295	50.44%
Soft Landscaping	$ 42,032	19.85%	$ 361,160	20.37%
Builders Contract Revenue	$ 56,800	26.83%	$ 517,600	29.19%
Total Revenue	**$ 211,703**	**100.00%**	**$ 1,773,056**	**100.00%**
Cost of Sales				
Material Purchases				
Material - Soil	$ 9,801	4.63%	$ 68,042	3.84%
Materials - Turf	$ 4,550	2.15%	$ 40,803	2.30%
Materials - Plants	$ 5,473	2.59%	$ 57,289	3.23%
Materials - Pavers	$ 25,448	12.02%	$ 183,346	10.34%
Materials - Pebbles / Rock	$ 5,367	2.54%	$ 60,065	3.39%
Materials - Weedmat	$ 739	0.35%	$ 9,151	0.52%
Materials - Letterboxes	$ 4,644	2.19%	$ 48,384	2.73%
Materials - Clotheslines	$ 9,690	4.58%	$ 87,791	4.95%
Materials - Concrete	$ 10,500	4.96%	$ 124,662	7.03%
Materials - Timber	$ 21,542	10.18%	$ 152,568	8.60%
Labour Expenses				
Labour - Wages & Salaries	$ 38,998	18.42%	$ 353,021	19.91%
Labour - Superannuation (Pension)	$ 3,705	1.75%	$ 33,937	1.91%
Labour - Insurance	$ 2,609	1.23%	$ 23,657	1.33%
Labour - Staff Amenities	$ 213	0.10%	$ 1,426	0.08%
Plant & Equipment Expenses				
P&E - Equipment Hire	$ 567	0.27%	$ 21,385	1.21%
P&E - Tools & Equipment < $300	$ 521	0.25%	$ 1,382	0.08%
P&E - Depreciation Expense	$ -	0.00%	$ -	0.00%
Motor Vehicle Expenses				
MV - Fuel & Oil	$ 1,036	0.49%	$ 18,306	1.03%
MV - Registration & Insurance	$ 3,544	1.67%	$ 8,234	0.46%
MV - Repairs & Maintenance	$ 1,331	0.63%	$ 4,805	0.27%
MV - Parking & Tolls	$ 186	0.09%	$ 1,511	0.09%
MV - Depreciation Expense	$ -	0.00%	$ -	0.00%
Total Cost of Sales	**$ 150,464**	**71.07%**	**$ 1,299,763**	**73.31%**
Gross Profit	**$ 61,239**	**28.93%**	**$ 473,292**	**26.69%**

Sam's Landscaping & Design

Profit & Loss Statement
April 202X

Gross Profit	**$**	**61,239**	**28.93%**	**$**	**473,292**		**26.69%**
Overhead Expenses							
Marketing Expenses							
Advertising	$	2,097	0.99%	$	24,970		1.41%
Branded Stationary	$	240	0.11%	$	10,480		0.59%
Entertainment Expenses	$	664	0.31%	$	7,524		0.42%
Total Marketing Expenses	***$***	***3,001***	***1.42%***	***$***	***42,974***		***2.42%***
Office Expenses							
Office Supplies	$	1,234	0.58%	$	7,299		0.41%
Postage	$	123	0.06%	$	1,235		0.07%
Telephone	$	1,247	0.59%	$	11,706		0.66%
Electronic Communication Exp	$	99	0.05%	$	909		0.05%
Total Office Expenses	***$***	***2,704***	***1.28%***	***$***	***21,149***		***1.19%***
Building Expenses							
Rent & Outgoings	$	4,433	2.09%	$	44,330		2.50%
Gas	$	288	0.14%	$	2,634		0.15%
Electricity	$	461	0.22%	$	5,186		0.29%
Water	$	276	0.13%	$	1,405		0.08%
Total Building Expenses	***$***	***5,458***	***2.58%***	***$***	***53,555***		***3.02%***
Professional Fees							
Accounting Fees	$	1,925	0.91%	$	28,565		1.61%
Dues & Subscriptions	$	834	0.39%	$	1,086		0.06%
ASIC License Fees	$	380	0.18%	$	380		0.02%
Total Professional Fees	***$***	***3,139***	***1.48%***	***$***	***30,031***		***1.69%***
Finance Expenses							
Bank Fees & Charges	$	205	0.10%	$	2,050		0.12%
Interest Expense	$	897	0.42%	$	8,966		0.51%
Insurance	$	704	0.33%	$	7,042		0.40%
Total Finance Expenses	***$***	***1,806***	***0.85%***	***$***	***18,058***		***1.02%***
Total Overhead Expenses	**$**	**16,107**	***7.61%***	**$**	**165,767**		***9.35%***
Operating Profit	**$**	**45,132**	***21.32%***	**$**	**307,526**		***17.34%***
Other Revenue & Expenses							
Asset Sales	$	-	0.00%	$	8,880		2.46%
Income Tax Expense	$	-	0.00%	($	12,458)	(	3.45%)
Total Other Revenue & Expenses	**$**	**-**	**0.00%**	**($**	**3,578)**	**(**	**0.20%)**
Net Profit / (Loss)	**$**	**45,132**	**21.32%**	**$**	**303,948**		**17.14%**

Sam and Beth took their time reviewing the more detailed report. Sam found it to be information overload as he tried to make sense of the impact of each account. The summarised report, however, was neat and concise and he could see how it would serve as a direction to which accounts he should look at in more detail when the need arose. They all agreed to use the summarised version and have the detailed version at hand for investigation.

To review, we outlined that the Profit & Loss Statement is a flow statement that reports on your business' earnings for a specific reporting period: month, quarter or year.

While Profit can be determined by deducting all expenses from revenue, we highlighted the benefits of categorising revenue and expenses into Operating Revenue, Cost of Sales, Overhead Expenses and Other Revenue and Expenses to determine the three levels of profit: Gross Profit, Operating Profit and Net Profit.

We learned that the importance of Gross Profit was to reach an absolute level in excess of Overhead Expenses to make an Operating Profit. We also learned that Operating Profit was generated from normal operations of the business whilst Net Profit included extraordinary items that occur outside your scope of management.

Here is a list of the things you should now know about the Profit & Loss Statement:

- The purpose of the Profit & Loss Statement is to calculate profitability;
- There are three levels of profitability: Gross Profit, Operating Profit and Net Profit;
- Revenue is the anchor on which all other elements are measured against;

- Cost of sales are expenses directly linked to revenue;
- Overhead expenses are the cost of maintaining the business model you have created;
- Other revenue and expenses are isolated as they are extraordinary and outside of your control;
- Gross profit margin is equivalent to the gross profit margin you earn on the sale of one unit;
- Gross profit margin can only be improved by raising revenue relative to cost of sales, reducing cost of sales relatively to revenue or increasing revenue and decreasing cost of sales;
- Gross profit margin cannot be influenced by increases or decreases in sales volume;
- Gross profit absolute value can be increased by improving the gross profit margin or increasing the sales volume;
- Overhead coverage occurs when the absolute gross profit is in excess of overhead expenses;
- Operating profit is the profit level we can influence with how we manage business activity;
- Other revenue and expenses are extraordinary and do not occur with normal trading;
- Net profit is the bottom line and the overall profit for a reporting period;
- Net profit is not net cash;
- Perfecting quoting or pricing your product is the key to a healthy Profit & Loss Statement.

CHAPTER 4

Without Stability, What's the Point

When Revenue Streams Fail, Where Are You?

Case Study—Sam's Balance Sheet

"Shall we discuss the Balance Sheet?" the bookkeeper suggested.

"How important is it? The Profit & Loss Statements tells us where we stand, right?" They had already been going for an hour, and Sam still needed to reach out to Simon about tomorrow's job. There was also the update he promised to Jake.

"The P&L only gives you a picture of one third of your cash situation. The Balance Sheet makes a good start at explaining the other two-thirds. Considering how tight your cash is, it's more important than the Profit & Loss Statement."

"Sam, sit tight. Jake can wait," Beth said, grasping his hand and giving it a squeeze. It had been a while since she had touched him inadvertently like that.

For long-term financial survival of your SME, financial stability is more important than profitability alone. When revenue streams fail, it is your SME's financial strength and depth of resources that will dictate how equipped your business is to survive a financial crisis.

Your SME's Balance Sheet reports on the infrastructure and resources your business model utilises to provide the core solution you are offering. Every SME should prepare and review their SME's Balance Sheet so they can make decisions that shore up financial strength and give their entity a fighting chance when adversity rears its ugly head.

The Balance Sheet is the second of the three core financial statements. It is more important than the Profit & Loss Statement because it reports on the business' financial stability. The stronger the Balance Sheet, the better equipped a business is financially to handle the impact of extraordinary events like natural disasters and economic slumps.

When a SME has a weak Balance Sheet, it is more reliant upon keeping business activity running on a day-to-day basis from the ongoing results of the Profit & Loss Statement. Living from one month's profit to the next is like the employee who lives from pay check to pay check and is not a long-term strategy for any successful and sustainable business.

Characteristics of the Balance Sheet

The Balance Sheet reports on a business' financial position. It summarises the assets the business owns, the liabilities or debts it has incurred and will settle at a future date, and the value of the owner's interest in the assets that exists at the point in time the Balance Sheet is prepared.

The Balance Sheet can be described as a position statement. It provides information at a particular point in time referred to as the balance date or reporting date. Unlike the Profit & Loss Statement that reports the elements from one point in time to another, the Balance sheet will report net values or the balance for each element at the reporting date. These net values or balances represent the net value for the lifetime of the entity's trading.

Like the P&L, the Balance Sheet should be prepared for each reporting period and as close to the last day of that reporting period as possible, be it monthly, quarterly or annually. It will provide information on the business' ability to settle its debts, the availability of cash, ownership of assets, and ultimately the owner's investment in their enterprise.

The small business owner often undervalues the Balance Sheet, yet it is the foundation which enables the SME to conduct business and provide the solution it offers. Even in its simplest form, the Balance Sheet is a better guide to financial stability and a business' longevity than the Profit & Loss Statement.

Cash vs Accrual Accounting

The Balance Sheet, like the P&L Statement, can be prepared on either a Cash Basis of accounting or Accrual Basis of accounting. When prepared on a cash accounting basis, the Balance Sheet will represent the balance of transactions at a particular date based upon the net consolidation of cash transactions for the life of the enterprise. When prepared on an accrual accounting basis, it will represent the balance of transactions at a particular date based upon the date the assets or liabilities were incurred.

The cash basis Balance Sheet is less sophisticated than the accrual basis version, however it still provides valuable information about the SME's financial stability. As with the Profit & Loss Statement, neither method is more accurate than the other; they present the same information using different calculations. The difference being the time transactions are recognised. Understanding the method used to prepare the Balance Sheet will help you decipher the information presented.

Quick checks to determine whether a Balance Sheet represents cash or accrual amounts is to verify whether accounts receivable or accounts payable balances are present on the report. These two elements are accrual accounting elements. If there are balances for one or both elements on the Balance Sheet, then it has been prepared on an accrual accounting basis.

When accrual accounting is taken to the extreme, the Balance Sheet becomes highly sophisticated with prepaid expenses, work in progress, accrued revenue and other accrual measurements. For the business owner and management of the SME's cash flow, such a sophisticated Balance Sheet is unnecessary. Remember, accrual amounts are not cash amounts.

The Format of the Balance Sheet

The premise of the Balance Sheet rests upon the following accounting equation:

Assets = Liabilities + Equity

The accounting equation can also be presented as:

Net Assets = Assets – Liabilities = Equity

The standard format of the Balance Sheet will have two columns: accounts and amount. The accounts column represents assets, liabilities and equity-type transactions, and will list the account name on the left-hand side of the page. These accounts discern the nature of the Asset, Liabilities or Equity and group like transactions together. The amount column will display figures aside of each of these accounts representing the balance of the transactional activity as of a particular date and for the life of trading of the entity.

Traditionally the Balance Sheet was reported with Assets on the left-hand side and Liabilities and Equity on the right-hand side. This format supports the first accounting equation where assets equal liabilities plus equity. The layout of this format showed the right-hand side had to be in balance with the value on the left-hand side. Besides being the financial statement that reports balances, it is also one reason it's called a Balance Sheet.

Today, the format of the Balance Sheet is focused upon reporting the net wealth of the entity at the reporting date. This format is based on the last accounting equation outlined above; net assets equals assets less liabilities equals equity. At a glance, this format reports on the business owner's claim on the assets of the business by deducting the claim held by third-parties. This allows the net consolidated transactions in equity for the life of the business to be balanced against the net assets owned by the business.

Case Study—Format of the Balance Sheet

Using Sam's Landscaping & Design's Balance Sheet information, the bookkeeper provided examples of both the traditionally formatted Balance Sheet and the format used today.

The traditional Balance Sheet is below.

Sam's Landscaping & Design

Balance Sheet

as at 30th of April 202X

ASSETS		**LIABILITIES**	
Current Assets		**Current Liabilities**	
Cash On Hand		VISA Credit Card Account	$ 4,359.70
Westpac Bank Account	$ 51,811	Accounts Payable	$ 131,213
Petty Cash	$ 500	Tax Liabilities	$ 9,770
		Payroll Liabilities	$ 10,052
Total Cash On Hand	**$ 52,311**	**Total Current Liabilities**	**$ 155,394**
		Non-Current Liabilities	
Accounts Receivable	$ 256,816	Vehicle Loans	$ 25,608
Inventory on Hand	$ -	Loan - Skid Steer Garden Tractor	$ 13,266
		Business Loan (Jake)	$ 200,000
Total Current Assets	**$ 309,127**	Land Loan	$ 60,000
		Total Long-Term Liabilities	**$ 298,874**
Non-Current Assets			
Land	$ 182,500	**Total LIABILITIES**	**$ 454,269**
Plant & Equipment at Cost	$ 288,697		
Motor Vehicles at Cost	$ 190,450	**EQUITY**	
Office Equipment at Cost	$ 8,752	Capital Contributions	$ 160,321
Furniture & Fixtures at Cost	$ 19,042	Drawings	($ 996,387)
Total Non-Current Assets	**$ 689,441**	Retained Earnings	$ 1,076,417
		Current Year Earnings	$ 303,948
		Total EQUITY	**$ 544,300**
Total ASSETS	**$ 998,568**	**Total Liabilities & Equity**	**$ 998,568**

The modern format of the Balance Sheet, most commonly used today, is below.

Sam's Landscaping & Design		
Balance Sheet		
as at 30th of April 202X		
ASSETS		
Current Assets		
Cash on Hand	$	52,311
Accounts Receivable	$	256,816
Inventory on Hand	$	-
Total Current Assets	**$**	**309,127**
Non-Current Assets		
Land	$	182,500
Plant & Equipment at Cost	$	288,697
Motor Vehicles at Cost	$	190,450
Office Equipment	$	8,752
Furniture & Fixtures at Cost	$	19,042
Total Non-Current Assets	**$**	**689,441**
Total ASSETS	**$**	**998,568**
LIABILITIES		
Current Liabilities		
VISA Credit Card Account	$	4,360
Accounts Payable	$	131,213
Tax Liabilities	$	9,770
Payroll Liabilities	$	10,052
Business Loan (Jake)	$	200,000
Total Current Liabilities	**$**	**355,394**
Non-Current Liabilities		
Vehicle Loans	$	25,608
Loan - Skid Steer Garden Tractor	$	13,266
Land Loan	$	60,000
Total Long-Term Liabilities	**$**	**98,874**
Total LIABILITIES	**$**	**454,269**
NET ASSETS	**$**	**544,300**
EQUITY		
Capital Contributions	$	160,321
Drawings	($	996,387)
Retained Earnings	$	1,076,417
Current Year Earnings	$	303,948
Total EQUITY	**$**	**544,300**

Sam studied each Balance Sheet. The traditional version reported the business had one million dollars in assets, and he was comfortable with that. He ran his eye down the list of assets and verified the right-hand side totalled the same figure as Debra had taught him to do. Overall, it looked fine to him.

When considering the modern format, he noticed the equity he held in business assets amounted to only $540,000. Pretty poor effort after five years of trading, considering they made profits of $300,000 this year alone.

Going over the liabilities, he was surprised to find he owed $355,000 to people outside the business, with $200,000 of it belonging to Jake.

He then reviewed the cash held at the end of April. The balance of $52,000 confirmed the obvious—he needed about $35,000 to settle the month's wages, which left very little to settle the other debts. The Balance Sheet still didn't seem to explain where all his cash was going.

Sam's mood slumped. He wondered what the Balance Sheet was truly reporting on his business. After what he learned about the Profit & Loss Statement, he was almost afraid to hear what lay beneath the surface of this second financial statement.

"Any questions?" Debra asked.

"If the Balance Sheet reports the cash balance at the end of the month, how can it explain anything more about our lack of cash other than the fact that there isn't any?"

The bookkeeper's smile showed she had been expecting this very question. Was he really so transparent?

"Cash flowing in and out of your business is represented in every element on the Balance Sheet, not just the cash at bank balance. You need to understand how these flows occur before you can release cash that is trapped on the Balance Sheet and maximise your cash balance."

"I have cash trapped on the Balance Sheet?"

"All businesses do. When you know where, you can manage it accordingly. The Balance Sheet goes a long way in explaining a lack of cash when you are making solid profits."

"Which is why the Profit & Loss is only one-third of the picture," Sam regurgitated, still in doubt about how the Balance Sheet could horde cash his business so desperately needed.

"Precisely."

Sam had nothing to lose, and he owed it to Jake to see what the bookkeeper had to say. In reflection, from what he learned about the Profit & Loss Statement he thought he understood so well, he was willing to proceed with the meeting.

Sam hoped he was about to discover the secret that eluded him for so long.

CHAPTER 5

The Recipe of Stability

Elements of the Balance Sheet

THERE IS MORE to the Balance Sheet than assets, debts and equity. When prepared accurately and consistently, it can provide you with intimate information about your business. It can report on the cash at your fingertips, if not yet in your bank account, track the level of wealth you have invested in your business assets, and summarise the resources of your business model.

Astute management of the Balance Sheet can release trapped cash reserves and allow you to maximise your return on investment without compromising your business' growth and stability. To do so, you need to understand what each element is telling you.

The Balance Sheet is primarily broken into three key elements: Assets, Liabilities and Equity. Assets and Liabilities are further broken down into current and non-current items.

> ***Current:*** *are items that are cash in nature or are expected to be converted into cash or extinguished with cash within a twelve-month period.*

> ***Non-Current:*** *are items expected to be converted to cash or extinguished with cash beyond a twelve-month period.*

Dividing the assets and liabilities into current and non-current categories allows the business owner to assess the entity's access to available cash and their ability to settle debts to third-parties. You can conduct analysis in the short-term by reviewing the current assets and liabilities and in the long-term by assessing total assets and total liabilities.

Only the Asset and Liability elements of the Balance Sheet are split into these two categories; Equity is not. Instead, equity is split into classifications that describe the movements of wealth held in your business. The equity section of the Balance Sheet also provides information on the SME's ability to provide a recurring cash return to the owner.

The key elements of the Balance Sheet are:

- Assets:
  - Current Assets;
  - Non-Current Assets.
- Liabilities:
  - Current Liabilities;
  - Non-Current Liabilities.

- Equity:
    - o Retained Earnings;
    - o Current Earnings;
    - o Capital Contributions;
    - o Drawings.

It is important to understand each element of the Balance Sheet and how it fits regarding your specific business model. We will now discuss each of the elements, the typical accounts classified within each element, and how cash is held, and sometimes trapped, within these accounts.

Assets

To provide an offering to customers, business owners will create a business model that serves as their business platform. This will require an investment in infrastructure in the form of physical assets that provide benefits to your business over the long term through the production or supply of the products and or services you sell. As you undertake day-to-day business activity, your business will also give birth to new assets that can be utilised to sustain and grow the offering of your product and/or services.

> ***Asset:*** *is an object, a right or a resource that is owned by a business representing a value which provides future benefits beyond a twelve-month period.*

In some instances, an asset is like an expense. To purchase an asset, cash is drawn out of the business, similar to an expense. However, an asset is distinct from an expense because it provides future benefits beyond a twelve-month period. An expense provides immediate benefits or benefits that will be consumed within a twelve-month period. An asset is reported on the Balance Sheet whereas an expense is reported on the Profit & Loss Statement.

Assets are physical items of future benefit purchased or created from day-to-day business activity. While they may not be cash held by your business today, they may represent future cash that will flow into your business.

Assets are the first item reported on the Balance Sheet.

On the traditional Balance Sheet, Assets are displayed on the left-hand side with a summation of the total value of all assets reported at the bottom.

In the modern format, it is the first element reported and is at the top of the statement. A summation of all asset account values is reported at the Total Assets line, which is used later on in the report to calculate the Net Assets of the business.

Previously, we mentioned that Assets can be classified further into Current Assets or Non-Current Assets, so we will now break this down.

Current Assets

Assets are represented at their cash value. Current Assets are assets representing cash you have ready access to and are available to manage your day-to-day business. An official definition is as follows:

> ***Current Assets:*** *assets that are cash in nature or likely to be converted into cash within a twelve-month period.*

For the SME, the most common items listed under Current Assets include cash at bank, inventory holdings, and accounts receivable. It is important to ensure the inventory and account receivable accounts are regularly converted into their cash value and transferred to the bank account.

Cash

A business will find it hard to operate without a bank account to facilitate cash receipts and the payment of bills and other obligations. It is important for the owner to keep their personal transactions separate from their business transactions and the cleanest and easiest way to achieve this it to run a business bank account to capture all cash transactions that are business related.

Every SME should have a cash at bank balance on the Balance Sheet. You recall the Balance Sheet is prepared at a particular point in time, customarily at month end or at year end. The amount listed on the statement will report the bank account balance at the date of the report.

Some businesses may hold more than one bank account. All bank accounts and balances should be listed under Current Assets if you have immediate access to the funds held. Where the business maintains more than one bank account or holds short-term cash investments, they will be listed under a sub-category of cash with a total for all cash holdings. The total of cash holdings represents all the cash available to your business to meet upcoming commitments.

For the start-up entity or a micro-business with a simple infrastructure, the cash at bank balance may be the only Asset reported on their Balance Sheet. For more sophisticated businesses with extensive infrastructure, cash at bank will be the first Asset reported under the classification of Current Assets with a total for all cash held.

To ensure the reported cash balances are correct, it is important to reconcile your business record's bank account with the bank statement activity reported by the bank. At best, this should be completed daily, but on a monthly basis at a bare minimum. This helps control your cash balance and installs confidence in the accuracy of the cash balance displayed in your accounting records and, subsequently, on your Balance Sheet.

Accounts Receivable

Not all entities will report account receivables (AR) on their Balance Sheet.

Accounts receivables will be reported on the Balance Sheet when you raise customer sales invoices on one date but receive payment at a later date. An accounts receivable balance will only be present on the Balance Sheet if the reporting date is between the date the invoice was raised and the date the invoice was paid.

When sales invoices are paid on the same day the invoice was raised, there will be no accounts receivable balance. For businesses that do not offer payment terms to their customers, no accounts receivable will be listed on the Balance Sheet.

> ***Accounts Receivable*** *(AR) is the debt a customer owes to a business, arising out of the normal course of business dealings. They are sometimes referred to as Debtors.*

The accounts receivable balance represents the total sum of outstanding invoices as of the reporting date. The balance represents the value of cash that will flow into the business in the coming days or weeks, dependent upon the credit terms granted.

As accounts receivables represent cash the business will receive within a twelve-month period, it is usually listed under Current Assets. In rare instances, due dates for accounts receivables may exceed twelve months. Only in these cases would accounts receivable be listed as Non-Current Assets.

Because accounts receivables represent cash, it plays an important part of any small business' cash management strategy.

The accounts receivable balance should be reconciled at the end of the month to ensure it captures only the sales invoices that have been raised but have yet to be paid. This will instill confidence that the balance truly represents cash the business will receive beyond the reporting date.

The accounts receivable balance should be kept at a minimum and only represent outstanding sales invoices not past the due date. Active collection activities should be conducted to recoup receivables that are overdue as soon as possible after the due date has passed.

Inventory

Inventory refers to the product you hold in reserve for resale to your clients. It is not usually applicable to service-based businesses unless they sell complimentary products to their services. Distribution, retail or manufacturing entities that maintain inventory levels will have an inventory balance reported on their Balance Sheet.

Distribution and retail businesses may wish to report categories of inventory representing the different products they sell or different categories. For manufacturing entities, the inventory balance can be split further into raw materials, work in progress and finished inventory.

For those businesses that sell products as the primary business activity, you will only have inventory listed on your Balance Sheet if you run an inventory register through your accounting database.

When you sell inventory, the cost attached to that item will be transferred to the Cost of Sales section of the Profit & Loss Statement at the date of the sale. If you do not run an inventory register, purchases of the product you sell will fall directly to Cost of Sales on the Profit & Loss Statement when you purchase it and there will be no inventory balance on the Balance Sheet.

Inventory reported on the Balance Sheet is usually product or stock stored in a secure facility or location. The destined purchaser of the product has not yet been identified, but a decision has been made to hold a certain volume of inventory or stock to facilitate immediate delivery to customers. As it represents future cash that will flow into the business within a twelve-month period, the inventory balance is reported under the Current Assets heading of the Balance Sheet.

Because the inventory balance represents cash, you should reconciled it at balance date. This can be done by ensuring all inventory purchases and sales have been recorded, returns captured and any damaged inventory removed. A cyclical count of the inventory items you hold can also be made and verified against the quantity held in your accounting records.

Maintaining an inventory register comes at a cost, and as a business you will need to weigh the benefits of tracking your inventory movements against the costs of doing so. Those able to invest in this accounting method must ensure the movements of inventory in and out of your business mirror the transactions that occur in the inventory account. This will ensure the inventory balance truly reflects the cost value of future sales that will flow into the business via cash receipts.

Non-Current Assets

Assets are represented on the Balance Sheet at their cash value. While Current Assets represent cash you have access to and is available for you to manage your day-to-day business, Non-Current Assets are not as liquid. Non-Current assets are usually physical assets needed by the business to produce or provide your product or service offering and generate revenue. They are not products you regularly sell.

Physical non-current assets are sometimes referred to as revenue-producing assets. Examples include manufacturing machines, operational machinery, furniture, computers and potentially a property your business owns and operates out of. Without these physical assets, you would struggle to produce or provide your offering to the market.

Sometimes, non-current assets can represent investments that will not, or cannot, be converted into cash for time extending beyond twelve months. For example, accounts receivables that are not expected to be settled in the coming twelve months will be reported under the Non-Current Assets of your Balance Sheet.

An official definition of non-current assets is:

> ***Non-Current Assets:*** *assets held in their current form and provide future benefits to the entity for a period longer than a twelve-month period. These assets are also referred to as fixed assets. The total of Non-Current Assets is also referred to as the Asset Base.*

The value of a non-current asset is usually cash outlaid by your business to secure ownership. Assets have the characteristic of being non-current when the benefit the asset provides is consumed over a period beyond twelve months and is unlikely to be sold or converted back into cash until the business extinguishes or replaces that future benefit.

As long as your business holds these assets, they will be reported on your Balance Sheet at their purchase value. When your business no longer has a need for them or replaces them, they can be sold for market value. The non-current asset will be removed from the Balance Sheet, and the cash received from its sale will be added to your cash reserves.

Non-Current Assets represent physical items or resources that hold or provide a future benefit that will be realised in excess of twelve months. For accounting purposes, only items fitting this description that are in excess of a set value are recorded as Non-Current Assets.

For example, a paper clip provides a future benefit that can be reused for years to come, so it holds a future benefit to the business. However, it isn't realistic or beneficial to record that paper clip as a non-current asset as its value is inconsequential and the cost to continue reporting it on the Balance Sheet far outweighs the benefits.

Assets that are below the value you set to determine what would constitute an asset are treated as an Expense. The cash value is not significant despite the future benefit it provides to your business, so the associated transaction is reported on the Profit & Loss Statement. Assets in excess of this set value are treated as a Non-Current Asset and are reported on the Balance Sheet.

I usually use the threshold of $1,000 to determine if I record an item that has a future benefit to my business. Assets above this threshold and of significant value are captured by my Balance Sheet and those that are below and inconsequential are reported on my Profit & Loss Statement. The threshold of $1,000 ensures I am only managing non-current assets that possess a significant cash value on my Balance Sheet.

Non-Current Assets represent an investment in your business. Non-current assets provide the infrastructure or foundation your business requires to offer your product and services to the market. In this sense, the total value of all your business' Non-Current Assets may also be referred to as your Asset Base.

Some entities will require a heavy investment in non-current assets. Manufacturing, construction or trade businesses will often have a substantial asset base to facilitate producing their product and/or providing their services. Service and retail businesses often have a lower-valued asset base. However, as every businesses structure is different, so too will be their Asset Base.

The most common categories of Non-Current Assets are outlined:

- ***Commercial Property:*** If you purchase land and buildings from which you conduct your business, the cash you paid for that land and buildings should be reported on your Balance Sheet to represent the value of your investment. It is sometimes listed as land and buildings.
- ***Motor Vehicles:*** Motor vehicles, commercial vehicles and trucks are usually recognised as motor vehicles on your Balance Sheet. A vehicle used by the director for business purposes or a truck owned by the business to transport product would be classified under motor vehicles.
- ***Plant & Equipment:*** Equipment used to manufacture, construct, provide a product or deliver a service is usually categorised as plant and equipment. An example would be a digger in a construction business or a canning machine in a food manufacturing company.
- ***Office Equipment:*** Equipment used by your office staff to conduct their tasks are usually classified as office equipment rather than plant and equipment. It can include computer hardware, printers, photocopiers, and other equipment used in the office environment.
- ***Office Furniture & Fittings:*** Whether you own your premises or have rented one, you will have invested some funds in fitting out your office and/or warehouse space. This will include items such as blinds, lighting, signage; items that are fixed to the premise. Office furniture such as desks, tables and chairs utilised by your staff within this space are also included as they are categorised as furniture rather than equipment.

Your business will not necessarily have all the non-current assets listed. The assets you have in your business depend on whether you are a service-based or product-based business and the business model you have created.

As the value of Non-Current Assets reported on the Balance Sheet represents the cash value of that asset, it is important to understand the effect upon the value of an asset over time. There are two types of assets in this respect: Appreciating Assets and Depreciating Assets.

Appreciating Assets: *are assets with cash values that increase over time.*

Depreciating Assets: *are assets with cash values that decrease over time.*

To ensure the Non-Current Assets reported on your Balance Sheet are represented at a conservative value, depreciating assets are depreciated periodically to recognise their decrease in value overtime. Depreciation expense represents the decrease in value for a twelve-month period and is recorded on the Profit & Loss Statement.

Accumulated depreciation is the total depreciation expense recorded on the Profit & Loss Statement since the date of purchase and represents the life-time reduction in value of a particular asset. Accumulated depreciation is recorded on the Balance Sheet and is deducted from the associated fixed asset purchase amount to determine the current value of that asset to the business.

From the list of non-current assets provided above, buildings, motor vehicles, plant and equipment, office equipment and office furniture and fittings are all depreciable non-current assets.

Implementing the task to recognise the depreciation in value of Non-Current Assets reported on your Balance Sheet does come at a cost. A fixed asset register will need to be maintained and an appropriate depreciation method will need to be applied to the asset for the term of its useful life.

These methods and procedures are outside the scope of this self-help guide, however it is important that you understand the values of Non-Current Assets represented on your Balance Sheet are at their cash purchase value and may no longer represent their true market value.

The aim of the Balance Sheet is to provide conservative values of your Non-Current Asset, so you know the realistic value of your Asset Base. Sometimes your non-current assets will appreciate in value rather than depreciate. An example is the land component of a commercial property.

Land purchased ten years ago, may be worth more today than it was the day you purchased it. When land is reported on your Balance Sheet at the cash value at the time of purchase, it is reported at a value less than its true worth.

You may be tempted to increase the value of this asset. However, it is not common practice to increase the value of individual non-current assets on your Balance Sheet. As values can fluctuate overtime, the general consensus is to maintain the purchase value on the Balance Sheet as this is the conservative value of the asset.

Only in special circumstances would such a revaluation be recorded. For instance, when the true value of the asset should be increased for the purpose of seeking outside third-party investment through refinancing or securing capital contributions.

For the SME's in-house management purposes, revaluation is unnecessary, however it is important to understand which assets may be of greater value than what the Balance Sheet reports.

For more information on depreciation and appreciation, and how it applies to Non-Current Assets reported on the Balance Sheet, please go to www.zephyrms.com/resources.

Total Assets

The last line in the asset section of your Balance Sheet is Total Assets. This line will provide you with the summation of the values of all your assets, both current and non-current.

Total Assets equals Current Assets plus Non-Current Assets

Total Assets = Current Assets + Non-Current Assets

For the traditionally prepared Balance Sheet, Total Assets will represent the balancing figure. For the modern format of the Balance Sheet, Total Assets will be the final figure relating to assets and be the starting figure in calculating the Balance Sheet's Net Assets.

Case Study—Sam's Assets

The bookkeeper referred to the modern format of their Balance Sheet assuring Sam and Beth were attentive before proceeding.

"I have done quite a bit of work on your Balance Sheet. We will focus on your business assets first, located at the top of the statement. Under Current Assets I've listed cash at bank (on hand) and accounts receivable, and under Non-Current Assets we have land, plant and equipment, motor vehicles, office equipment, and furniture and fixtures at cost. All of these assets are represented at the cash amount you paid to purchase them.

"Regarding the cash on hand, I have reconciled it up to the end of April so your accounting records are in agreement with the actual cash balance in your bank account. The balance on the Balance Sheet also includes the five hundred dollars float you have in your petty cash tin.

Sam's Landscaping & Design

Balance Sheet - Assets
as at 30th of April 202X

ASSETS		
Current Assets		
Cash on Hand	$	52,311
Accounts Receivable	$	256,816
Inventory on Hand	$	-
Total Current Assets	**$**	**309,127**
Non-Current Assets		
Land	$	182,500
Plant & Equipment at Cost	$	288,697
Motor Vehicles at Cost	$	190,450
Office Equipment	$	8,752
Furniture & Fixtures at Cost	$	19,042
Total Non-Current Assets	**$**	**689,441**
Total ASSETS	**$**	**998,568**

"For accounts receivable, Beth and I confirmed the balance only represents the sales invoices that were not paid as of the last day of April. All invoices paid previously have been matched with their cash receipt and we can now identify which invoices are overdue."

"We have over $250,000 tied up in unpaid customer invoices?" Sam blustered, unable to reconcile this to the figure he had in mind. He would have sworn it was no more than $100,000 they were carrying.

"About $180,000 relates to what you invoiced this month and the two invoices from March which are on sixty-day terms. The value of unpaid invoices amounts to $78,000. While just under thirty-five has been received since the last day of April, there is $43,000 over thirty days past due," Debra said.

"Ouch."

"Some of these invoices we thought had been paid, like Bruce Sanders and Meghan Munns, but we went through every cash deposit in the bank account both since we did these jobs and a

month prior, and we couldn't find the money. Debra gave me some ideas about how to address this with the customers, and I've called them and organised payment plans. Most of it will be paid off by the end of June," Beth explained. "There is, however, the $10,000 Thrifty Investments are refusing to pay."

"We'll never get a dime." Sam was still angry they would have to absorb the full cost of landscaping for two sites where landscaping was not a part of the build specifications. Thrifty Investments provided them with the sites, and Sam had several emails confirming the request for the landscapes to be completed and by when. It was more Thrifty Investments' fault than theirs.

"Is there any chance they may be willing to pay half? You'd only have to write off $5,000 rather than the full ten," Debra suggested.

"I'll call them," Sam said decisively. "What else?"

"You have no inventory. Beth mentioned you order materials on a job-by-job basis and have it delivered to the site either the day before or the morning of the job, so it is expensed upon delivery."

"We lose less that way, believe it or not. It just took too much time to manage it from here and the additional cost to transport it was killing us. What we lose at the site is almost nothing."

"Good, managing inventory can cause a lot of headaches, and you need to ensure you have good control mechanisms in place to manage it tightly," Debra agreed. "That's it for current assets. At the end of April, you had $309,000 in cash held and in cash coming in.

Sam could only wonder where it was. In his customer's pockets was his best guess.

"For the non-current assets, I made sure only the cash values for the assets you're holding in workable condition are included. I removed assets sold in previous years, as well as the trailer in the yard that's ready for the scrap yard. Beth mentioned you replaced it a couple of months back so the new trailer's included in the total.

"Your Balance Sheet reports that you have an Asset Base of about $690,000. Your total assets are almost one million and thirty percent are cash or almost cash. Once again, this confirms

you have solid cash inflow and don't have too much cash tied up in long-term assets. Also, you don't have any long-term assets that only have a cash value benefit because all your non-current assets are revenue generating assets and are working for you."

"Glad to hear it."

"Shall we look at the liabilities?"

Sam nodded. This is where Jake's loan would rear its ugly head. However, seeing that they had over $300,000 in cash and near-cash current assets, shouldn't they be in a position to just pay it out?

Liabilities

To make money, one needs to spend money. In a business scenario, we often do not have that money to begin with, so we may borrow funds to smooth the flows of money through our businesses. These funds can be borrowed from third parties with a commitment and obligation to repay the money at a later date. Such borrowings are reported on the Balance Sheet under the element of Liabilities.

On the modern Balance Sheet format, Liabilities are the next main element. Liabilities represent the value of all debts and obligations your business has committed to.

When you started out on the SME journey, you may have acquired a business loan in order to finance the purchase of non-current assets or build the infrastructure you utilise in the delivery of the product and or services. The value of this business loan represents the debt you will have to pay at some point in the future.

As you conduct business on a day-to-day basis, you will continue to accrue additional debt and settle some of the previous debt you acquired. At any point in time your business will have obligations and debts that need to be settled at a future date. These liabilities will be represented on the Balance Sheet as the balance that has yet to be paid at reporting date.

Liabilities can be defined as follows:

> ***Liabilities:*** *Liabilities are existing financial obligations to external parties other than the business owner, which are to be settled in the future by the business.*

To settle debts or obligations, you will need to relinquish some of your cash. Payment can be made from cash in your bank account, by converting some almost-cash assets into cash, or by transferring ownership of an asset of the same value to the creditor. Either way, settlement of an obligation or debt will result in a reduction of your held assets. It is important to understand the total level of obligations and debt your business has accumulated in respect of the total assets you own.

Like Assets, Liabilities are split into Current Liabilities and Non-Current Liabilities. Splitting liabilities into these categories enables the reader of the Balance Sheet to assess how easily or quickly a business is able to settle their current and non-current debts and obligations.

Current Liabilities

Liabilities are represented on the Balance Sheet at their cash value. Current Liabilities are financial commitments or debts that represent the value of cash you will have to part with to extinguish the obligation against you. Current Liabilities can be defined as follows:

> ***Current Liabilities:*** *are existing financial obligations or debts to external parties other than the business owner, that are expected to be settled within a twelve-month period.*

Current Liabilities are short-term debts or payments your business needs to make in the coming weeks and months. Examples of current liabilities include the payment of credit card balances, supplier accounts, payroll obligations, tax obligations and business loans expected to be paid in full within twelve months.

Credit Card Facilities

Credit Card facilities represent a short-term loan that is expected to be repaid within twelve months. Of course, it is best practice to settle your credit card debt on a monthly basis, but sometimes this can linger when funds are short. Since the expectation is that the credit card balance will be paid as soon as possible to minimise interest charged, the credit card balance is reported as a Current Liability.

Any interest charged on a credit card balance is recorded as an Expense and will be captured on the Profit & Loss Statement. The credit card balance that includes any interest charged is represented on the Balance Sheet as the total amount you owe to the credit card provider at reporting date.

Your credit card account should be managed as your cash at bank account is managed. It is important to reconcile your accounting record's credit card balance with the credit card's statement activity reported by your bank to ensure the Balance Sheet is accurate. This reconciliation should be completed at least on a monthly basis and at best on a daily basis. This will assist you in controlling the accuracy of the credit card debt displayed in your accounting records and stemming out-of-control spending before it becomes problematic.

Accounts Payable

Not all entities will report accounts payable on their Balance Sheet.

Accounts payable will be reported on the Balance Sheet when you process supplier invoices on one date and pay the invoice at a later date. For suppliers offering payment terms to you, it is astute practice to record this invoice in your database when you receive it. At any point in time, as long as your supplier invoice processing is up to date, you can assess what you owe on a supplier by supplier basis. This will assist you with managing your cash by paying the invoices as they fall due.

An accounts payable balance will not be reported on the Balance Sheet in two instances. If all supplier invoices processed have been paid in full by reporting date, there are no outstanding supplier invoices and there will be no accounts payable balance. If supplier invoices are not processed and purchases are recorded via cash payments, there will be no accounts payable balance.

> ***Accounts** Payable (AP) is the debt you owe to your supplier, arising out of the normal course of business dealings. It represents cash that will flow out of your business when payment is made. It is sometimes referred to as Creditors.*

The accounts payable balance on the Balance Sheet represents the total sum of supplier invoices that are outstanding and have yet to be paid as of the reporting date. The accounts payable balance represents the value of cash that will flow out of the business when you settle the supplier's invoices.

Since accounts payable represents cash leaving the business, you should ensure the payment is made within the payment terms provided and when you have sufficient cash to do so. You do not want to upset essential suppliers by paying outside their payment terms. By ensuring that all monthly purchases and cash payments have been processed as they are received, you can assess the level of cash payments required before due dates and, if necessary, implement collection activities regarding converting outstanding accounts receivables into cash.

You should also ensure that you do not pay supplier invoices until their due date. When you pay suppliers that have granted your business credit terms, you do your business a disservice by paying them ahead of time. The longer you can hang onto your cash, the better. However, this is a fine line that requires management and planning.

Ideally, your cash management strategy should be to hang onto your cash as long as possible without upsetting valuable suppliers. To delay payment to core supplies could cause delays of crucial products and services the delivery of your offering depends on, resulting in missed sales and reduced revenues.

Payroll Obligations

Your business will probably grow to the point where you need to employ staff. Whilst some start-ups will require this from the outset, many entrepreneurs start the journey solo or with a partner. Once you are ready to take the leap and start recruiting people into your team, you have two ways in which to accomplish it.

Contractors or consultants can be hired for one-off projects or recurring projects that are small and don't substantiate enough hours to warrant direct employment. Such contractors and consultants will run their own businesses and can manage payment by providing you with a supplier invoice. As mentioned above, supplier invoices are processed to accounts payable and are extinguished from accounts payable when paid in full.

I have worked for some entities that fulfill their needs by employing contractors and subcontractors. These businesses established a date these contractors would be paid and, in a sense, created a contractor and subcontractor payroll date.

Even in these instances the invoices provided are processed through accounts payable and extinguished on the payroll date the business specified.

Supplier invoices from subcontractors, contractors and consultants are not considered payroll obligations. Payroll obligations are monies owed to employees because of their contracted employment. As soon as your business starts employing staff, you are likely to accrue annual leave, sick leave, obligations for pensions and payroll taxes.

Most payroll obligations are reported on the Balance Sheet under Current Liabilities. These accounts will display at balance date the amount you owe to either the employee, service provider or tax agency associated with the payroll obligation.

It is good practice to reconcile the payroll obligations at the time you process your payroll. You can ensure the payroll obligations are consistent and correct from one payroll to the next. When the Balance Sheet is prepared you can be confident that the payroll obligations are relevant and accurate.

Tax Obligations

Taxation is an unavoidable consequence of running a business, but it is not all bad news. If your business is paying taxes, it is generating profits. And profits are good.

When you run a small business, particularly a profitable one, there is no avoiding the demon of taxes. Taxes are usually region specific, so I will not be mentioning specific taxes that may be imposed on your business. In general, taxes include value added or consumption taxes, income taxes, fringe-benefit taxes, payroll taxes, sales taxes, state taxes, federal taxes, etcetera.

When such obligations arise, they will represent a liability and are usually reported on the Balance Sheet under Current Liabilities, for they are usually payable relatively soon after they arise. From the moment the obligation exists, the tax obligation will be present on the Balance Sheet until it is extinguished in full.

Non-Current Liabilities

Liabilities are represented on the Balance Sheet at their cash value. While Current Liabilities represent cash you must pay to third-parties in a short period of time, Non-Current Liabilities are not as liquid. Non-current liabilities are long-term obligations and debts that need to be extinguished or settled in the long-term future.

Non-Current Liabilities can be defined as:

> ***Non-Current Liabilities:*** *are existing financial obligations to external parties other than the business owner, that are expected to be settled over a period that is longer than twelve-months.*

The most common example of Non-Current Liabilities are loans to third parties.

Loans

Starting a new enterprise takes funding. Growing an established entity also requires funding, whether in the form of purchasing additional assets or covering the increase in operating expenses whilst awaiting an increase in revenue. This funding is sourced from within the business itself, from the business owner, or from external third parties. When finance is provided by a third party or the owner upon the condition that it will be repaid within a defined period, this is represented on the Balance Sheet as a loan.

One point to remember about any loan is while they provide funds in the form of cash today, lump-sum repayment or instalments require a draw down on future cash reserves.

To meet the terms of any loan, you will need to ensure your business generates enough cash on an ongoing basis to repay the loan at the designated time for the life of the loan.

A short-term loan is one that will be repaid within a twelve-month period and is represented as a Current Liability. A long-term loan is one that will be repaid over a period longer than twelve months and is classified as a Non-Current Liability.

Loans are made up of two components—the original principal and an interest component. There are two main types of loans: interest only loans or principal loans, which are characterised by the payments made against them.

In either case, interest charges are considered an Expense and will be captured on the Profit & Loss Statement, decreasing the month's Net Profit. The principal, which is the balance represented on the Balance Sheet, will be reduced as principal payments are made. The impact on the Profit & Loss Statement and Balance Sheet is determined by the terms of loan.

Interest only loans will require regular payments of interest only. More often than not this is monthly, however it can be quarterly or even annually if specified in the terms of the loan. The principal amount of the loan will not change from one reporting period to the next, so the loan balance on the Balance Sheet will not change from one reporting period to the next as there is no principal component in the interest. The interest payment will affect the Profit & Loss Statement, reducing net profit.

Equity loans, or interest and principal loans, may require a regular repayment amount which constitutes part principal and part interest. The principal loan amount will change from one reporting period to the next. The loan balance represented on the Balance Sheet will progressively decrease by the principal amount in the repayment. As for interest only loans, the interest component of a principal and interest repayment will impact the Profit & Loss Statement and reduce net profit.

The loan accounts should be reconciled regularly to confirm all interest and principal amounts are captured correctly. This will ensure the Profit & Loss Statement reports the interest and correct net profit, and that the Balance Sheet represents the correct outstanding loan principal.

When the due date of a long-term loan starts to fall within the next twelve months, the loan will no longer be classified as a Non-Current Liability but a Current Liability. Changing the classification becomes important when assessing if you have enough liquid current assets to pay the obligation at the time it is due.

Payroll Obligations

Sometimes payroll obligations arise that are expected to be paid at a time that is beyond twelve months. In Australia, long service leave is one example where the obligation is accrued regularly but is only paid when the employee takes their long service leave after ten years of employment with the same company.

The long service leave obligation is accrued on an ongoing basis and would be classified as a Non-Current Liability. Similar to a business loan, when it is expected that the employee will take their long service leave in the coming twelve months, it would then be reclassified as a Current Liability.

Total Liabilities

The next line on the Balance Sheet is Total Liabilities. This is the summation of all Current Liabilities and Non-Current Liabilities.

On the traditionally formatted Balance Sheet, Liabilities will appear on the top left-hand quadrant of the report with a line for Total Liabilities. This gives a visual representation of the percentage claim third parties have upon the assets of the business.

On the modern formatted Balance Sheet, Liabilities are reported under the Total Assets line. The total liabilities are deducted from the total assets to calculate the net assets of the business. The Net Asset total becomes the balancing figure of the Balance Sheet.

Net Assets equal Total Assets Less Total Liabilities

Net Assets = Total Assets – Total Liabilities

Case Study—Sam's Liability Dilemma

Debra explained that liabilities are split into current and non-current, as were the assets. This allowed them to determine the total value of debt that needed to be settled in the months immediately following April. These were listed under the current liabilities heading. The balance of the equipment loans were listed under non-current liabilities, as was the loan from Sam's father for the land, since both would be settled in full after April the next year.

Below is an extract of Sam's Landscaping & Design's Balance Sheet. It shows the total assets held by the business and the liabilities owed, and it also calculates the difference between the two, referred to as net assets.

Sam's Landscaping & Design Balance Sheet - Net Assets as at 30th of April 202X		
Total ASSETS	**$**	**998,568**
LIABILITIES		
Current Liabilities		
VISA Credit Card Account	$	4,360
Accounts Payable	$	131,213
Tax Liabilities	$	9,770
Payroll Liabilities	$	10,052
Business Loan (Jake)	$	200,000
Total Current Liabilities	**$**	**355,394**
Non-Current Liabilities		
Vehicle Loans	$	25,608
Loan - Skid Steer Garden Tractor	$	13,266
Land Loan	$	60,000
Total Long-Term Liabilities	**$**	**98,874**
Total LIABILITIES	**$**	**454,269**
NET ASSETS	**$**	**544,300**

Sam inspected the spread of liabilities—credit card balance, supplier invoices not yet paid, tax and payroll liabilities, and Jake's loan. "Shouldn't the business loan from Jake be under non-current liabilities?"

"Prior to his phone call it would have been. However, since he's asked for it to be repaid within the next two months, it is now a current debt."

"I understand the payroll liabilities, but what are the tax liabilities for? We paid the income tax earlier this year."

"That is the net GST payable, or value added tax payable, for the month of April. It isn't due until July," Debra explained.

"Okay, but why isn't that reported on the Profit & Loss Statement?"

"Value-added taxes are not a revenue or expense item. It is a collection on sales and you receive a refund for it on expenses.

The Profit & Loss Statement reports the net value of revenue and expenses only. On the Balance Sheet, value-added taxes are an accrual balance, so the tax is recorded at the time of each transaction it applies to. When you lodge the return with the tax department and pay the net amount, the balance will be cleared to zero. May's Balance Sheet will have April and May's tax debt, and June will have the full quarter. In July, the balance from the end of June will be brought to zero when the tax is paid."

Sam deliberated for a moment. "So, this is telling me I have to find $355,000 in the next forty days?"

"Yes."

Sam cursed. "Sorry," he spluttered.

Catching Beth's eye, the sickening dread of reviewing his assets he'd swept aside returned. He hoped it wouldn't get any worse.

Equity

Equity is the third, and final key element reported on the Balance Sheet. Equity represents the wealth of the business owner regarding the assets their SME possesses and utilises in the generation of their revenue. The wealth of the business owner is equated to Net Assets of the SME.

When you start the SME journey, the alternative to obtaining funds through a business loan is to contribute the capital yourself to facilitate the purchase of non-current assets and equipment, and acquire the infrastructure you utilise to deliver your product and/or services.

On a progressive basis, net profits are earned via your business activity, adding to your equity, and when losses are made, your equity will reduce. When your business activity reaches a sufficient capacity, you will start drawing a wage or a portion of the profits your SME has earned. This is drawing on the equity in your business.

Equity is often overlooked as being an element that needs to be managed. Some business owners see it as just the balancing element on the Balance Sheet. However, equity, just like your business' profits, assets and liabilities, should be managed on a progressive basis to ensure you retain a healthy claim over the assets of your business.

What is Equity?

Equity on the Balance Sheet is like the equity you have in property you own outright or have a mortgage against. The property reflects your asset, the mortgage reflects the liability, and the remaining value is what you own of the property: equity.

> ***Equity:*** *represents the owners' interest in the business' assets and residual profits; meaning what portion of the business's total assets the owners own after they have taken into account total liabilities. It is also referred to as 'Owner's Equity'.*

As equity on the Balance Sheet reflects the value of the assets that you as business owner have a claim to, the Balance Sheet is sometimes referred to as a Wealth Statement. Equity is the wealth the SME provides the business owner.

On a traditionally formatted Balance Sheet, Equity is reported on the bottom right-hand quadrant under Total Liabilities. The top quadrant of the right-hand side represents third party claims on your business assets, and the bottom right-hand quadrant represents the business owner's claim on the business' assets.

Total Assets equals Total Liabilities plus Equity

Total Assets = Total Liabilities + Equity

On the modern format of the Balance Sheet, Equity is represented as an element separate from Total Assets and Total Liabilities. Total Equity is reported as being equal to the Net Assets of the business. Net Assets are equal to Total Assets, less Total Liabilities. Total Equity becomes the balancing figure of the Balance Sheet.

Net Assets equals Total Assets Less Total Liabilities

Net Assets = Total Assets – Total Liabilities

Where;

Net Assets equals Total Equity

Net Assets = Total Equity

It is important to understand how Total Equity is calculated. Each equity account needs to be managed differently and contributes to the total of equity differently.

The most common equity accounts of the Balance Sheet are:

- Capital Contributions,
- Drawings,
- Retained Earnings, and
- Current Earnings

Another equity account may be an asset revaluation reserve. This equity account will appear when a revaluation of the business' assets has been undertaken and the increase in the equity of those assets is recorded and captured in the

Balance Sheet. To be an accurate representation of an increase in equity, such a revaluation would only be recorded such that all depreciating assets are also depreciated periodically. To record a revaluation of your assets without depreciation being calculated and recorded would result in inflating total assets beyond that which would be considered conservative.

We will not discuss asset revaluation or depreciation further as it is beyond the scope of this guide.

Now we'll look at each type of equity account in detail. Keep in mind that the balance shown on the Balance Sheet will represent a lifetime balance and not just the total of transactions of the current twelve-month period. It is worthwhile to compare the balances from one year to the next on at least an annual basis to fully understand how your entity's financial stability has changed, grown, or in some cases, declined.

Analysis of equity can also be achieved by preparing a fourth financial statement called an Equity Statement. This financial statement looks at the balance of equity at the beginning of the reporting period, then details the movements of the four equity accounts during the reporting period to arrive at the closing balance of equity as reported in the Balance Sheet at the same reporting date.

I have excluded detailed analysis of this financial statement because reading and interpreting the equity section of the Balance Sheet, along with the movements captured by the Cash Flow Statement, is more than sufficient for the SME entrepreneur to manage the equity in his/her business. The Cash Flow Statement will be reviewed in detail during chapters seven, eight and nine.

The first equity account we will look at is Capital Contributions.

Capital Contributions

> ***Capital Contributions:*** *are contributions made by the business owner in the form of cash or assets. They have been contributed to the business upon the basis that there is no expectation of repayment like a loan facility.*

When the business owner provides money to the business without expectation of the money to be repaid, it is recorded as a Capital Contribution and not a loan. These funds or assets can be provided at any time, but more often than not will occur at the commencement of the business, representing the cash or assets required to help fund infrastructure needed to produce or provide the core products or services.

Capital Contributions are displayed in the Balance Sheet as a positive value and will be added to the overall value of Total Equity, resulting in an increase. The balance of the Capital Contributions account will represent at the report date the total value of all assets the business owner contributed to their business over the life of the business.

Retained Earnings

> ***Retained Earnings:*** *alternatively called Retained Profits, are the consolidated net profits (loss) resulting from the business' operations from the inception of operating activity to the end of the last full financial year. This line directly links the Balance Sheet to the Profit & Loss Statements of previous years.*

Retained Earnings, or Retained Profits, are the total net profits your business earned over the life of the business until the end of the previous financial year. At the end of each financial year, the annual Net Profits reported on the Profit & Loss

Statement are transferred to the Retained Earnings balance. This clears the Profit & Loss Statement to start the following financial year with zero amounts, whilst the life-to-date profits of your business are reported on the Balance Sheet.

The Retained Profits balance on the Balance Sheet will be the same for every subsequent month of the financial year. At the end of the next financial year, that year's profits are added to Retained Earnings and so on. In effect, the profits calculated on the Profit & Loss Statement do not disappear at the end of the year. They are added to the equity you hold in the business and continue to be reported each month.

If annual net losses occur, the Retained Earnings balance is reduced. More often than not, the Retained Earnings balance is a positive value and will increase total equity. If your business is in a start-up phase and minimal trading has resulted in net losses, then this value will be negative and will reduce total equity. For an established business, if consecutive net losses have been incurred and they are in excess of total net profits made over the life of the business, then Retained Earnings will also be negative and more accurately called Retained Losses.

A heavy loss position on a continuing basis is not sustainable in the long-term and radical strategic decisions will need to be actioned to improve your business' profitability and the health of the Profit & Loss Statement. Healthy profits will flow onto the Balance Sheet and will also improve the state of your wealth in your business when equity increases in value.

Current Earnings

Current Earnings, or Current Profits, is the element that links the Profit & Loss Statement to the Balance Sheet during the current financial year. Current Earnings reflect the current net profits earned from your business activity. Similar to Retained Profits, Current Profits are added to the wealth of your SME and therefore should be added to the equity you hold in your SME.

For a Balance Sheet to be complete it must report the up to-date Current Profits for the financial year. The Balance Sheet depends on the year-to-date profits and therefore will need a Profit & Loss Statement to be prepared first. Whilst a P&L can be prepared in isolation, a complete Balance Sheet cannot.

> ***Current Earnings:*** *alternatively called Current Profits, are the net profit (loss) resulting from the business' operations for the current financial year. This line directly links the Balance Sheet to the Profit & Loss Statement for the current financial year.*

Current earnings are the consolidated net profit, which is the year-to-date net profit you have earned for the current financial year. The financial year will start with a zero balance, as does the Profit & Loss Statement. Net profits made are accumulated month by month. By year end, the Current Earnings balance equates to the net profit for that financial year.

If your business activity results in a net loss for a reporting period, that net loss is deducted from the year to-date summation of net profits. If you incur a net loss every month of the year, and the amount is high enough to offset any net profits made, then your current earnings will be negative and will reduce the overall equity you hold in your business.

Drawings

Whilst our objective is to make the world a better place by offering our solution, in the end we need to be paid for our efforts. It is critical that what your business pays you is what your business can afford. When you withdraw too much, your business becomes starved of cash. Cash is like oxygen to a business, for without it the wheels of business activity are hindered and chances for growth without extensive borrowing becomes impossible. When starved of cash on a long-term basis, a profitable and healthy business can die.

There are two ways we can be paid from our businesses. We can either receive a wage and run it through the payroll process we apply to employees, or we can withdraw funds from the business bank account. In some cases, I have witnessed both methods being applied concurrently.

When we draw assets out of our businesses, the transaction is recorded as drawings.

> ***Drawings:*** *are withdrawals of cash or assets by the owner. Drawings usually represent the equivalent of net wages paid to the owner or payment of private expenses from business funds.*

Drawings represent the amount or value of assets the owner has taken out of or withdrawn from the business and used for personal purposes. Drawings, in this sense, are the opposite of Capital Contributions. For example, Drawings could constitute cash withdrawn from the business bank account, payment of personal expenses from the business bank account, or even the withdrawal of an asset to be used for personal purposes.

When calculating total equity, drawings are deducted from capital contributions and total earnings to reduce the value of total equity. If drawings exceed the capital contributions and earnings of the business, the total equity will be negative.

It is crucial to business success that the level of drawings is managed to ensure there is enough equity retained in the business to provide the financial stability required for day-to-day trading and growth objectives.

Total Equity

Total equity is the summation of all equity elements.

Total Equity equals Capital Contributions plus Retained Earnings plus Current Earnings less Drawings

Total Equity = Capital Contributions + Retained Earnings + Current Earnings - Drawings

When Total Equity is positive, it represents the value of the claim the business owner has over the business' total assets. When Total Equity is negative, the claim third parties have to your business is greater than the value of your business' total assets. In this case, the business is insolvent and remedial action needs to be undertaken immediately or the business will fail.

Case Study—Sam's Ownership

"Let's look at what you own of your assets," Debra said.

Sam's Landscaping & Design

Balance Sheet - Equity
as at 30th of April 202X

NET ASSETS	**$**	**544,300**
EQUITY		
Capital Contributions	$	160,321
Drawings	($	996,387)
Retained Earnings	$	1,076,417
Current Year Earnings	$	303,948
Total EQUITY	**$**	**544,300**

Sam inspected the equity section of the Balance Sheet while Debra explained the accounts listed. Whilst Capital Contributions and the Retained and Current Earnings amounted to over one and a half million dollars, cash or assets drawn out of the business were almost one million dollars by themselves.

Sam felt somewhat relieved to see that he owned half a million of the business' assets. It could have been worse.

The value of Capital Contributions seemed accurate. They provided only $50,000 when they started the business, using the bulk of Jake's money to buy the start-up assets. In the first few years, they occasionally took $10,000 off the mortgage to settle business bills, but that stopped when they started building their dream home.

Concerning Retained Earnings, they had been trading for five years, which averaged approximately $200,000 in profits per year. This also seemed right since they'd doubled in size during the past two years and only had the contracts for the two builders for eighteen months. This was a record year, for profits anyway.

When Sam came across the level of drawings, he baulked. "Drawings can't possibly be right. We haven't drawn a wage for months."

"I understand you built a home a couple years ago and you've just finished furnishing it," Debra highlighted delicately. "Many of those bills were paid by the business."

Sam sighed. Beth's dream home was definitely turning into a white elephant. "Yes, we went way over budget. The loan just covered the build and we've had to pay for the furnishings ourselves. But I thought it was only the occasional bill."

Debra slid a report across the table. It showed a list of transactions, all of which related to the furnishing of their home. A great deal more than the 'occasional bill' had been run through the business. In the past two years, they had withdrawn close to $400,000. It was no wonder there was no cash. Embarrassed, Sam avoided the bookkeeper's eye as she continued explain.

"Drawings are only one reason you have little cash. You are growing rapidly. In the past two years your growth has been

above thirty percent, which you are funding internally, and that will always put a strain on your cash flow. We've identified some funds trapped in receivables and we can look at ways to improve payment management of your supplier invoices. However, you do need to reduce the amount you are drawing out of the business. You should also avoid having personal bills paid directly. We can work out what your business can afford to pay you so you can withdraw one amount per month, then work from there."

Sam nodded, still sheepish.

Debra tried to console him. "This is more common than you think. Tax accountants and tax departments have business owners focus on their profitability because that is where their interest is. They'll tell you you're having a great year because you're bringing in record net profits of $400,000, but fail to tell you that profitability is only one third of the financial picture.

"When you look at your Profit & Loss Statement in isolation, it appears reasonable to draw out assets at the level you've been taking. However, there is always cash trapped on the Balance Sheet, or often cash is required for items other than expenses. You need to take this into account when determining what your business can afford to pay you.

"The trick is making the cash on the Balance Sheet work for you and not drag you down the rabbit hole of doom. To achieve this, you need to prepare a Balance Sheet every time you prepare a Profit & Loss Statement, and also understand how each of these elements on the Balance Sheet relate to one another, just as we did for the P&L."

"So, there's hope we can turn this around?"

"Of course!" Debra's words exhibited no doubt. "You have a viable business, Sam. Once you understand how cash flows through your business and how to manage it to your benefit, you'll be surprised at how much cash you can generate.

To maximise the value of the Balance Sheet for your business, reconcile the Asset, Liability, and Equity accounts on a periodic basis to ensure all transactional activity during the accounting period has been captured in the final balance.

By reconciling the Balance Sheet elements, you also ensure your Profit & Loss Statement is accurate and reflects all activity that has occurred for a period. Often the correction of transactions on the Balance Sheet that have been missed or recorded in error will impact revenue or expense accounts.

For example, by processing a sales invoice that was missed to correct the inventory balance, you will alter the Revenue line and the Cost of Sales line on the Profit & Loss Statement. By ensuring that the balances on the Balance Sheet are accurate, you are by default improving the quality of information on your Profit & Loss Statement.

By starting with the preparation of your Profit & Loss Statement, you are ensuring the Net Profits for the year are reported accurately at Current Earnings on the Balance Sheet. Reconciling the accounts on the Balance Sheet serves as a check that every transaction has been captured and you can fine tune the P&L accordingly. Once the Balance Sheet has been reconciled in full, you can confirm that both the Profit & Loss Statement and Balance Sheet are accurate and truly reflect the business activity for the reporting period.

In the following chapter, *The Backbone of Your Entity*, we will look at the relationship between the Balance Sheet elements. Analysis will unlock the reasons you have no cash when you are generating healthy profits.

CHAPTER 6

The Backbone of Your Entity

No Backbone, No Survival

THE BALANCE SHEET is the backbone of your business. When a crisis occurs and your business activity is compromised, revenue streams and subsequent profits will decline or vanish, testing the financial stability of your business.

The Balance Sheet summarises the cash and physical assets your business has in hand, outlines what you owe to third parties and what equity you own. The stronger the Balance Sheet, the stronger your financial stability. This strength will determine how well you will survive any crisis when it arrives, for at some point it will.

Like the Profit & Loss Statement, it is important to understand the Balance Sheet elements and their relationship with one another. Once you understand these relationships, you place yourself in a position to manage your resources and obligations to strengthen your financial position.

Before we look into the relationship between the Balance Sheet elements, we will summarise the differences between the Profit & Loss Statement and the Balance Sheet. We have touched upon them previously, but it is worth pulling them together to refresh them.

How does the Balance Sheet differ to the Profit & Loss Statement?

There are three fundamental differences between the Profit & Loss Statement and the Balance Sheet:

- flow versus position,
- earnings versus wealth, and
- independence versus dependence.

The Profit & Loss Statement is a flow statement. This means it captures the value of transactions from one point in time to another, which is usually a month, a quarter or a year. All transactions that occur outside of the defined period are included on the previous statement or the following statement. At the start of the reporting period, elements will be at zero. The value of the elements reported on the Profit & Loss Statement are a sum of all the transactions that have occurred during the reporting period.

In contrast, the Balance Sheet is a position statement. It represents the balance of transactions for the life of trading at a particular point in time. That point in time is the date the Balance Sheet is prepared and is usually the last day of the reporting month, quarter or year. At the beginning of the reporting period, the Balance Sheet elements start with the balance that existed at the end of the previous period. Transactions during the reporting period are added and subtracted from this balance to bring us to the balance at the end of the reporting period. This is the value reported against the element on the Balance Sheet.

Rather than being a summation of transaction values, the balance represents the net value of all transactions relating to the element after a lifetime of trading.

For instance, cash at bank on the Balance Sheet will not indicate the total amount of cash that has passed through the business over time. It will indicate the balance of cash in the bank account at the end of a reporting period. At the start of the period, the cash balance has been carried forward. During the reporting period, cash incoming will have increased the cash balance whilst cash outgoing will reduce the cash balance. At the date the Balance Sheet is prepared, the cash balance existing at that date will be reported.

All Balance Sheet elements—Assets, Liabilities and Equity—are treated like the cash at bank account. Each element's balance at the date of preparing the Balance Sheet is reported on this statement. This is one reason this statement is called a Balance Sheet.

The second difference between the two statements refers to earnings and wealth. The Profit & Loss Statement shows net earnings over a particular period, whereas the Balance Sheet is a statement of net wealth at a point in time. To calculate the wealth of the business, you need to take into account the earnings over the life of the business. The calculation of wealth on the Balance Sheet therefore depends on the Profit & Loss Statement.

Previously we mentioned that elements of Current Earnings and Retained Earnings on the Balance Sheet reported on the profits as calculated by the Profit & Loss Statement. All net profits from the time trading began until balance date are recorded under Retained and Current

Earnings on the Balance Sheet, increasing the equity of the business owned by the business owner. Net losses will reduce the balance under Retained and Current Earnings.

This brings us to the third difference between these two statements. Whilst a business can prepare a Profit & Loss Statement in isolation and independent of other reports, the Balance Sheet depends on the Net Profits or Earnings as calculated on the Profit & Loss Statement. In most situations a business will need to prepare their business' P&L first.

In rare circumstances, a business will possess Balance Sheet elements, however do not have any transactions affecting the Profit & Loss Statement. This will usually occur for a start-up entity with a heavy investment in assets that need to be in place, or has secured a business loan before trading has begun. When trading begins, revenue is earned and expenses are incurred. A Profit & Loss Statement will need to be generated to enable the preparation of a fully encompassing Balance Sheet.

For a true representation of an enterprises' financial status from an operational and financial position perspective, it is good practice that both the Profit & Loss Statement and Balance Sheet Statement are prepared on a monthly basis. Cash is represented in all elements of both statements and when only one statement is prepared, the full financial picture is not being reported.

Once you prepare Balance Sheets, you will need to be able to recognise if it is reporting a healthy financial position or not.

A Healthy Balance Sheet

So, what does a healthy Balance Sheet look like?

A strong Balance Sheet indicates the wealth of the owners is significant. It should also report increases in wealth over time through ongoing profits. An unhealthy Balance Sheet exists when the wealth of the owners is insignificant and is being compromised by excessive debt and/or ongoing losses. The extent of the impact of excessive debt and obligations can be assessed in the short-term and in the long-term.

The premise of the Balance Sheet rests upon the following calculation:

Total Assets equals Total Liabilities plus Equity

Total Assets = Total Liabilities + Equity

We can assess the health of the Balance Sheet and subsequently the health of your business' financial stability by undertaking an assessment of the relationship between the elements on the Balance Sheet.

- Current Liabilities can be measured against Current Assets,
- Non-Current Liabilities can be measured against Non-Current Assets,
- Total Liabilities can be measured against Total Assets, and
- Drawings can be measured against Total Earnings.

These four assessments provide an analysis of the Liquidity of your business.

Liquidity

Liquidity is the ability of a business to meet its debts and obligations from cash and cash assets they hold. The level of liquidity in a business can be measured on the face of the Balance Sheet. By measuring liabilities against the asset value, we can get a sense of their ability and how quickly they can pay their debts.

> ***Liquidity*** *is the ability of a business to meet its debts and obligations from cash and cash assets they hold.*

Debt is a necessary evil in any business. However, there is a fine line between an acceptable level of debt and what is detrimental to the operations of your business. Too much debt can over burden your business, whilst too little debt may mean you are missing out on growth opportunities you could take advantage of. Generally, the business owner wants to own more equity in their business than third-parties do. But what level of debt is acceptable?

From a top-level perspective, it is considered healthy for an SME to have a level of debt of forty percent or lower in value than the Total Assets of the business. This allows access to enough debt to enable growth in the form of expanding your business model and acquiring additional assets, increasing business activity and meeting day-to-day requirements but will not bog it down with the burden of extensive repayments and borrowing costs.

When Total Liabilities are above forty percent of Total Assets held, your business will experience cash flow issues. At first, your business will show signs of not being able to finance growth from internal resources. At higher levels, it will struggle to meet day-to-day commitments, possibly impacting business trading.

A more detailed analysis can be conducted by measuring Current Liabilities against Current Assets. Remember that current elements can be converted into cash or extinguished by cash within a twelve-month period. The higher Current Assets are over Current Liabilities, the better your SME's liquidity in the short-term.

When Current Liabilities are greater than the value of Current Assets, a business is likely to struggle meeting their short-term debts and obligations. Cash flow issues will arise and the day-to-day trading of the business will be compromised. When Current Liabilities are lower than Current Assets, a business is unlikely to have issues with meeting their day-to-day commitments.

The ideal position is to have a level of Current Liabilities equal to or less than the value of Current Assets. In this position, the business has cash or assets that can be converted into cash in the immediate future that can settle the current liabilities in full.

Non-current assets are often purchased with the use of external finance. External finance can come in the form of capital contributions by the business owner or through financial lenders external to the business. Sometimes a general business loan may be obtained by using the physical assets already held by the business as collateral and surety that the loan will be repaid.

Finances from external lenders are reported under Non-Current Liabilities.

It is logical to measure Non-Current Liabilities against Non-Current Assets considering this debt was most likely incurred in the purchase process or is secured by the value of the physical assets already held and will be repaid over a period in excess of twelve months. To maintain a healthy position for Total Liabilities against Total Assets, a healthy position of Non-Current Liabilities would be thirty percent of Non-Current Assets.

In the table below, we have summarised the levels of healthy liabilities for an SME.

Healthy Status of the Balance Sheet	
Element	**%**
Current Liabilities	<=100% of Current Assets
Non-Current Liabilities	<=30% of Non-Current Assets
Total Liabilities	<=40% of Total Assets

The premise of the Balance Sheet is based upon the calculation of Net Assets equating to Total Equity. Remember, net assets are calculated by deducting total liabilities from the value of total assets and is also the same value as equity an owner holds in their business. From the above discussion, a healthy position for equity would be sixty percent or higher.

Though it is important to assess an SME's liquidity position from the relationship of liabilities to assets, these are not the only elements on the Balance Sheet that impact the ability of the SME to meet its debts and obligations. Equity elements also impact cash flow and a business' liquidity. Whilst capital contributions representing assets brought into the business will improve an SME's liquidity situation, drawings can compromise it, particularly if they are excessive.

Drawings on the Balance Sheet

Cash is like oxygen. Without cash, a business cannot breathe. When we draw cash or assets out of our business, that cash or assets are no longer available for the business to use. When excessive drawings occur, businesses can be starved of cash and set on a road to ruin.

Having worked with and within small businesses for over twenty-five years, I have paid witness to profitable and viable businesses being suffocated by business owners drawing excessive amounts of business capital. When this occurs, the SME does not have the capital or cash to grow to their full potential, and sometimes to meet day-to-day commitments. When it becomes chronic, it has the potential to derail the most profitable and cash generating SME.

Please don't misunderstand me. It is important that business owners receive a return on the investment of their time and heartache of running a business and have enough to pay the essential cost of living. However, the level of drawings taken from the business needs to be managed and measured, as does every other element on the Balance Sheet and Profit and Loss Statement.

It is necessary to determine the level of drawings your business can afford to ensure you are not removing the level of capital it needs to keep the trading wheels turning.

When the affordable level of drawings is insufficient for the business owner to accept or even survive upon, changes need to be made to improve the availability of cash in your business so you can draw an amount you deserve and deem appropriate. This may mean managing the cash flows affecting your Balance Sheet, increasing the volume of business activity, or implementing strategies that improve your gross margin and profitability.

Drawing more cash and assets than what your business can afford is not sustainable in the long run.

When assessing the level of drawings a business can sustain, I look at two analysis.

The first is on the Balance Sheet. We can assess the level of drawings taken over the life of your entity and assess whether they are too high or are within what your business can afford. We can also assess from Current Earnings what level of drawings your business can afford based on current activity.

The second analysis can be conducted from the Cash Flow Statement and will be discussed in proceeding chapters.

Drawings are reported under Equity on the Balance Sheet. They are represented at their life-time value and provide the total value of cash and assets the business owners have withdrawn from the business and represents capital no longer available for use by the business.

We can assess the life-time level of Drawings against the Total Earnings to-date. The level of drawings is considered healthy and sustainable at thirty percent or lower. When drawings are in excess of thirty percent of Total Earnings, then drawings are excessive and a drain on your SME's cash reserves.

We can measure the level of life-time drawings with the following calculation:

Total Drawings divided by Total Earnings

Total Drawings / Total Earnings

where;

Total Earnings equals Retained Earnings plus Current Earnings

Total Earnings = Retained Earnings + Current Earnings

When drawings are at thirty percent or less of Total Earnings, you ensure seventy percent or more of the business earnings are reinvested into your business. Cash and other assets are available to meet day-to-day obligations, including taxes, and reserves of cash are available to facilitate growth.

When drawings exceed thirty percent, they encroach on the cash your business needs to meet growth objectives. When drawings exceed sixty percent of your total earnings, cash flow issues will extend to struggling to meet day-to-day expenses and obligations.

To determine the level of drawings your SME can afford, we turn to Current Earnings. Current Earnings, or Current Profits, is the current profitability level of your business. By annualising the year to-date profit of your entity, you can apply thirty percent to calculate the level of drawings you can extract from your business annually without compromising growth opportunities or your ability to meet obligations.

Affordable Drawings equals Current Earnings divided by months to-date multiplied by twelve multiplied by thirty percent

Affordable Drawings = Current Earnings/ months to-date x 12 x 30%

The Affordable Drawings amount calculated using the method above is a gross amount and includes the portion you will have to pay for personal taxes. You can decide whether to withdraw this now or at the time of having to pay the tax, however it would make sense to leave these funds in your business cash reserves so your business has access to them until that time.

But drawings are cash, and profits are not cash. Why do we use profits to calculate drawings?

Profits are not one hundred percent cash, but they contribute to the operating cash your SME generates. The Balance Sheet is only one way to assess what level of drawings is affordable for your SME. The second and equally important analysis is the assessment done from the Cash Flow Statement, which will be discussed in the following chapters.

I have often done this calculation for clients. Some are devastated by the need to reduce their level of drawings to set their business on a path of sustainability. However, all is not lost. We discussed in chapters one through to three how to maximise the profitability of your business. In chapters four through to six, we discussed how cash can be trapped on the Balance Sheet and how to release it. By implementing deliberate and focused strategies you can improve and manage your cash flows, maximize profits and subsequently put your SME in a position to pay you what you deserve.

Alternatively, you may be surprised by how much your business can afford to pay you. The value calculated by the above formula may be more than what you have been drawing out of your business. However, it does not mean you should withdraw cash up to this level. The astute business manager will withdraw not only the level of drawings their SME can afford, but only the level needed to support their family financially. It is always better to leave cash in your business than to withdraw it, for once it has been taken out and is no longer available to your business, it is gone.

Your Finance Engine is a cash machine. As long as cash remains within the structure of the Finance Engine and you manage the flows of cash through your business prudently, it will reward you by generating more cash.

Case Study—The Liquidity of Sam's Balance Sheet

Sam studied the full Balance Sheet. He grew nervous when Debra mentioned she conducted a 'health analysis' upon it. He was also eager to understand what made her so sure they could turn their cash position around.

"I pulled together the following table," Debra continued. "It summarises the current and non-current totals along with drawings as reported on the statement and gives us a good snapshot of

your business' level of liquidity. I removed the business loan from current liabilities so you could see that excluding the loan, your business liquidity is quite good at fifty percent.

"Repaying the loan in June and classifying it as a current liability, compromises your liquidity, pushing it to one hundred and fifteen percent. However, once that's resolved and you have secured refinance, the loan will move to non-current liabilities and you'll return to fifty percent. The key will be staying on top of your accounts receivables and making sure they're paid by the due dates.

"Non-current liabilities are light at fourteen percent of non-current assets. Total liabilities are high at forty-five percent. This will be the same once you have the refinance loan in place, however, as you repay the refinanced loan this will improve with every instalment, as long as you finance your growth internally and don't increase your borrowings."

Sam's Landscaping & Design - Balance Sheet Targets		
Current Assets	$	309,127
Current Liabilities w/o Loan	$	155,394
% of Current Assets		50.27%
Current Liabilities with Loan	$	355,394
% of Current Assets		114.97%
Non-Current Assets	$	689,441
Non-Current Liabilities	$	98,874
% of Non-Current Assets		14.34%
Total Assets	$	998,568
Total Liabilities	$	454,269
% of Total Assets		45.49%
Total Earnings	$	1,380,365
Life-time Drawings	$	1,076,417
% of Total Earnings		77.98%
Annualised Current Earnings	$	364,737
Affordable Annual Drawings (30% of Annualised Current Earnings)	$	109,421

"We could do that?" Sam asked, running his hand through his hair. A sense of relief awash with the possibilities fell over him.

"Definitely, as long as you get your drawings under control and streamline your cash inflows with cash outflows. Your business is like a machine's engine—you need cash to flow through it in the right direction for it to operate well," Debra said. "Otherwise, your Finance Engine will breakdown."

Sam smirked, recalling the level of drawings. There was always a catch.

"Drawings for the life of the business are at seventy-eight percent," Debra continued. "This will be a red flag to the bank. The tax department also doesn't like it when you run personal expenses through the business, so set yourself up with a monthly or weekly set withdrawal and manage your personal expenses outside of the business."

Sam inspected the percentage of drawings on the table and caught sight of the affordable drawings Debra calculated. "Are you saying we can draw a yearly wage of a hundred and nine grand?"

"Yes," Debra said with caution. "That is what your business can afford based on your current earning power. However, I strongly suggest you get drawings as low as possible, at least until it frees up your cash flow and the strategies you implement bear fruit.

"Over time, and particularly in light of the increase in profits the past eighteen months, the life-time drawings percentage will improve. The actions we discussed regarding the Profit & Loss Statement will also help, and there are a few things you need to do with the Balance Sheet elements that will improve things even further."

They turned to discussing strategies they could implement regarding the Balance Sheet elements. Over a second coffee and thirty minutes later, they came up with a list of cash management strategies, most of which they could implement immediately.

Below is the list of strategies they developed.

- *Reconcile the bank account weekly;*
- *Issue sales invoices at job completion;*
- *Implement collection strategies to bring in outstanding accounts receivables and maintain future levels of debt at minimum levels;*

- *Reintroduce a thirty percent deposit required before projects begin;*
- *Enter supplier invoices weekly;*
- *Use accounts payable report to determine when supplier invoices fall due;*
- *Pay supplier invoices on due date or within ten days after due date;*
- *Determine the best day to pay suppliers based upon cash levels and due dates;*
- *Negotiate thirty-day credit terms with current cash suppliers;*
- *Use credit cards only when necessary and not for mainstream suppliers with credit terms;*
- *Implement a capital expenditure policy that enables smaller assets to be paid from internal cash and seek finance only for larger assets;*
- *Set drawings at $80,000 per year, paid monthly;*
- *Avoid running personal expenses through the business;*
- *Prepare Balance Sheet on a monthly basis;*
- *Review Balance Sheet on a monthly basis;*
- *Analyse liquidity using liquidity table metrics.*

Sam and Beth reviewed the list of cash management strategies they identified. As with the list they had compiled from the Profit & Loss Statement, they were both pleased that the list of changes was manageable and could be implemented quickly with ease.

Customising the Balance Sheet

As with the Profit & Loss Statement, the Balance Sheet can be customised to assist with specific decisions you must make on a day-to-day basis. This will save further investigation because the information you require at hand is on the face of the Balance Sheet report.

Whilst the format of the Balance Sheet is usually dictated by the accounting software used, you can usually group and consolidate similar elements to provide another level of information. For example, your cash accounts can be grouped together to give a total of all cash holdings. This will allow you to process the information provided swiftly and in context, without having to apply manual interpretations.

Below, using our case study, we have customised the Balance Sheet for Sam's Landscaping & Design.

Case Study—Customising Sam's Balance Sheet

Sam inspected the customised Balance Sheet Debra prepared, noting the increase in the details of his liabilities.

Sam's Landscaping & Design

Balance Sheet
as at 30th of April 202X

ASSETS		
Current Assets		
Westpac Bank Account	$	51,811
Petty Cash	$	500
Total Cash On Hand	**$**	**52,311**
Accounts Receivable	$	256,816
Total Current Assets	**$**	**309,127**
Non-Current Assets		
Land	$	182,500
Plant & Equipment at Cost	$	288,697
Motor Vehicles at Cost	$	190,450
Office Equipment	$	8,752
Furniture & Fixtures at Cost	$	19,042
Total Non-Current Assets	**$**	**689,441**
Total ASSETS	**$**	**998,568**
LIABILITIES		
Current Liabilities		
VISA Credit Card Account		
Visa - XXXX XXXX XXXX 5632	$	2,221
Visa - XXXX XXXX XXXX 3269 T1	$	426
Visa - XXXX XXXX XXXX 3254 T2	$	1,084
Visa - XXXX XXXX XXXX 1236 T3	$	628
Total VISA Credit Card Account	***$***	***4,360***
Accounts Payable	$	131,213
Tax Liabilities		
GST Collected (VAT Payable)	$	21,170
GST Paid (Vat Receivable)	($	11,401)
Income Tax	$	-
Total Value Added Tax Liabilities	***$***	***9,770***

Sam's Landscaping & Design

Balance Sheet

as at 30th of April 202X

Payroll Liabilities	
PAYGW (Employee Taxes) Liability	$ 6,347
Superannuation (Pension Fund) Liability	$ 3,705
Total Payroll Liabilities	***$ 10,052***
Business Loan (Jake)	$ 200,000
Total Current Liabilities	**$ 355,394**
Non-Current Liabilities	
Loan - HiLux 4x4 (FRX372)	$ 2,709
Loan - HiLux 4x4 (FRX374)	$ 2,307
Loan - HiLux 4x4 (FRX374)	$ 2,408
Loan - Ford Falcon Ute (XFD991)	$ 18,185
Loan - Skid Steer Garden Tractor	$ 13,266
Land Loan	$ 60,000
Total Long-Term Liabilities	**$ 98,874**
Total LIABILITIES	**$ 454,269**
NET ASSETS	**$ 544,300**
EQUITY	
Capital Contributions	$ 160,321
Drawings	($ 996,387)
Retained Earnings	$ 1,076,417
Current Year Earnings	$ 303,948
Total EQUITY	**$ 544,300**

Sam found value is separating out the credit card balances, allowing him to see how much each team was using the facility. The spread of the equipment loans was also useful.

Debra had broken down the spread of cash so Sam would know where his cash was being held. She also provided more detail regarding their tax and payroll obligations, as they each had different due dates.

Sam was as surprised with what he learned from his Balance Sheet as he was when they reviewed the Profit & Loss Statement. He was now convinced that he and Beth needed to make a point of preparing both statements each month and spend time thoroughly investigating them. His interest in what the Cash Flow Statement could provide piqued.

They took a break for lunch and reconvened in an hour to review the Cash Flow Statement. Sam had skimmed some of the later chapters in her book, Discover Your Finance Engine. Considering what he'd learned so far, he wondered how much more he'd been missing all these years.

We have explained that the Balance Sheet reports on your business' financial stability by presenting the assets, liabilities and equity of your business. We have had a detailed discussion on the difference between Current and Non-Current elements and deep-dived into the natures of the most common accounts classified under these elements.

We provided metrics to assist with the measurement of a healthy Balance Sheet from a liquidity standpoint and from the position of earnings. We have also looked into the relationship of the Balance Sheet to the Profit & Loss Statement and the dependency the Balance Sheet has to the determination of profit and subsequent equity.

Below is a list of all the things you should now know about the Balance Sheet:

- The purpose of the Balance Sheet is to assess your financial stability;
- Assets are a right or item that will provide future benefits to your business;
- Liabilities are debts or obligations that your business has to settle with cash or another asset;
- Liabilities represent third-party interests in your business assets;
- Equity is what you own of the assets held in your business;
- Assets and Liabilities are classified into Current and Non-Current items;
- Current items are cash, or will be converted to cash or extinguished with cash, within a twelve month period;
- Non-Current items are a right or physical item that can be converted into cash, or an obligation that is extinguished with cash beyond a twelve-month period;
- Liquidity is the ability of your SME to settle its debts and obligations;
- Current Liabilities can be measured against Current Assets to assess your SME's short-term liquidity;
- Non-Current Liabilities can be measured against Non-Current Assets to assess your SME's long-term liquidity;
- Total Liabilities can be measured against Total Assets to assess your SME's overall liquidity;

- Life-time Drawings should be at or below thirty percent of your Total Earnings;
- Current Drawings should be at or below thirty percent of your Current Earnings;
- When debt is excessive, you reduce your level of liquidity;
- When drawings are excessive, you reduce your level of liquidity;
- Cash can be trapped on the Balance Sheet;
- Management of the Balance Sheet elements is required to ensure trapped cash is at a minimum.

It is now time to look at the statement that serves as a bridge between the Balance Sheet and the Profit & Loss Statement. It is the most important statement of the three and is the Cash Flow Statement.

CHAPTER 7

Without Oxygen, What's the Point

Cash Makes Your Enterprise Breathe

Case Study—Sam's Cash

Everyone returned from lunch, refreshed and ready to tackle the Cash Flow Statement. Sam's eagerness to continue was obvious.

"Debra, what exactly is the point of the Cash Flow Statement?" Sam asked. "The Balance Sheet provides us with the cash balance, we can assess our capability to meet our short-term and long-term obligations by measuring assets against liabilities, and we can keep a track of our drawings. What more can the Cash Flow Statement bring to the table?"

"Cash allocation, Sam. The Profit & Loss Statement can measure whether your business activity is profitable. The Balance Sheet can assess how liquid and financially stable your business is. But it's the Cash Flow Statement that tells you where all your cash is going.

"You have to know the activities that drive your cash flows before you can implement effective change. As you mentioned when we were discussing the strategies to implement from the Balance Sheet, you need to change some financial habits to improve your cash situation. What doesn't materialise on the other two statements becomes glaringly obvious on the Cash Flow Statement."

"Okay then, we'd better have a look."

Cash is King. Without cash, your SME cannot breathe.

Have I said this before? In case you haven't grasped that yet, which is unlikely, I will say it again.

Cash is oxygen for your business.

Without cash you cannot trade on a day-to-day basis, you cannot grow your business and just as importantly, you cannot afford to support yourself financially.

Cash drives the Finance Engine of your SME. When we start our commercial endeavours, we need cash to establish the infrastructure we utilise to create and deliver our products and/or services. We need cash to pay our day-to-day expenses and obligations, and to grow our businesses to reach our ultimate visions for our SME. Without cash, our SME will not survive.

It is how we allocate the cash and maintain sufficient reserves which determine the level and speed of success of our entities. Not profits or financial stability, but cash. By allocating every dollar of cash with forethought and direction, you can subsequently maximise the increase in your SME's profitability and secure its financial stability. The key is understanding how your SME consumes cash compared to how it regenerates cash.

Let's look at an example of spending one dollar in a business that generates a forty percent Gross Profit Margin. The consequences or implications of that dollar spent will differ depending on whether it was spent on a consumable element or a regenerating element. Below we will demonstrate the impact of where you allocate your dollar:

- If you are making a gross profit margin of forty percent, one dollar spent on a cost of sale expense on your Profit & Loss Statement will generate a gross profit return of sixty-seven cents. If sixty-seven cents are reinvested in a cost of sales expense it will generate a further gross profit of forty-five cents. Invested again, it will return thirty cents. While a short-term investment, one dollar invested and the subsequent return reinvested twice more will result in one dollar and forty-two cents. A forty percent return on your original one-dollar investment will occur.
- If you earn a fifty percent return on assets each month, one dollar spent on an asset will generate fifty cents in net profit every month for the life of that asset. This is a long-term investment in your business that will generate recurring income. The more cash we can channel into assets that offer a return, the greater our SME's profitability.
- If one dollar was spent on the repayment of debt, it is no longer available to the business. If the debt was incurred to purchase an asset, then we would receive a future return on the asset. If the debt was incurred to prop up liquidity, we are borrowing against future profits. Hence, by the time we pay back the loan, it is from profits we have earned in the past. While debt serves a place in the SME, it must be taken with great consideration of the benefits.
- One dollar spent on drawings is gone forever. The dollar is consumed at the time of withdrawal. When cash is withdrawn from the business for personal purposes, it is no longer available to the business and is gone forever.

From the above analysis, it's most beneficial to invest our one dollar in our SME's assets or in cost of sale expenses that generate revenue and net profits. The third best option is to spend it on debt that enables past profits. The worst option is to consume the one dollar by withdrawing it out of the business entirely.

It is important to understand where our cash is being allocated in our SME so we can maximise our returns. The more cash we re-invest into our businesses, the better foundation upon which we can trade on a day-to-day basis and from which we can grow the entity. It is imperative that every SME manages the cash flowing into their entity and the cash flowing out, ensuring it is being put to its best use for the SME's present viability and for a sustainable future.

Hence the need for the Cash Flow Statement.

While the Balance Sheet is undervalued by small business, the Cash Flow Statement is ignored to the small business' detriment. The Cash Flow Statement is the most important of the three core financial statements. If you prepare only one statement, it should be this one. Without cash the small business would not survive, so it is more important to manage cash flow than profits or wealth.

The Bridge Between Statements

While a Cash Flow Statement can be prepared in isolation, for effective cash management, this statement should be prepared alongside the Profit & Loss Statement and the Balance Sheet. The most important characteristic of the Cash Flow Statement is that it forms a bridge between the Profit & Loss Statement and Balance Sheet.

The Cash Flow Statement captures all cash-based transactions. It does not capture new transactions. Every transaction that is reported on the Cash Flow Statement has already been captured on the Profit & Loss Statement or the Balance

Sheet. It merely represents the movement of cash between the other two statements, providing you with an overall summary of your business' trading from a cash perspective.

Like the Profit & Loss Statement, the Cash Flow Statement is a flow statement, or a period statement, because it provides information from one point in time to another. This span of time, or reporting period, is usually a month, a quarter or a year and the statement is prepared for the same period the Profit & Loss Statement is prepared.

The Cash Flow Statement will report revenue in the form of cash receipts and expenses regarding cash payments. It will also capture cash movements on assets purchased and sold, liabilities taken or paid, and equity contributions and drawings. It is a summary of both the Profit & Loss Statement and Balance Sheet regarding cash movements.

The Cash Flow Statement is linked to the Balance Sheet in that the closing cash balance on the Cash Flow Statement will be the same as reported in the cash at bank line of the Balance Sheet. The Cash Flow Statement explains how the cash at bank balance at the start of the period arrives at the closing balance at the end of the period by reporting on the cash that was deposited and withdrawn.

It is how these cash transactions are presented on the Cash Flow Statement which provides the purpose for preparing this statement.

The Cash Flow Statement reconciles the opening and closing balance of the bank account by reporting on the movements of cash in and out of the SME. Cash transactions are summarised into Operating Activities, Investing Activities and Financing Activities. The purpose of these categories allows the business to identify where their greatest needs for cash exist and ultimately explains the Net Cash Increase or Decrease in your cash balance resulting from trading during a reporting period.

The Net Increase or Decrease of the cash balance can be referred to as the Cash Burn Rate. Whether the cash flow has increased or decreased in a reporting period is discerned by comparing the closing cash balance to the beginning cash balance of the reporting period. If cash is being retained by the business, the cash burn rate is positive and the business' cash balance will increase. If the cash burn rate is negative, more cash is being used than received. Should a negative cash burn rate exist over multiple reporting periods, there is a likelihood the business will run out of cash.

Cash vs Accrual

Financial statements can be prepared on one of two accounting methods: Cash Basis of accounting or Accrual Basis of accounting. The accounting method is irrelevant when we are considering the Cash Flow Statement.

The Cash Flow Statement only represents and summarises transactions that represent movements of cash. It is not concerned with the accrual nature of transactions, which is the time at which an obligation, expense or revenue is raised or earned. Accrual methods follow transactions at the date of raising invoices or credits. All transactions that effect the Cash Flow Statement are captured at the time the cash movement occurs.

As a rule, if a transaction has not run through a cash account, it will not be captured by the Cash Flow Statement. The Cash Flow Statement can therefore be said to always be prepared on the Cash Basis of accounting.

Format of the Cash Flow Statement

There are two formats in which the Cash Flow Statement can be prepared: the indirect format or the direct format. While both differ regarding how the transactions are captured, the category totals should not differ much, if at all.

Indirect Format

The indirect format of the Cash Flow Statement is a formal reconciliation between the Profit & Loss Statement and the Balance Sheet to extract the cash movement during a month or year. It is the method used by accountants and tax practitioners and involves comparing opening balances with closing balances of the elements on the Balance Sheet. This in effect isolates the movements between one reporting period to the next.

Preparing a Cash Flow Statement under this method will require the preparation of both a Profit & Loss Statement and a Balance Sheet beforehand. For a micro-business that has limited resources, this may be a challenging task. In that case, such a micro entity would benefit from preparing a Cash Flow Statement on the second of the two formats: the direct format.

Direct Format

The direct format is the compiling of the cash transactions directly from the bank transaction listing and can be done in isolation of preparing a Profit & Loss Statement and Balance Sheet.

This is the easiest format and the one I suggest a micro or small business to undertake. By downloading your bank accounts transactions on a daily basis, you can build your Cash Flow Statement progressively through the month and assess the total of all cash transactions at the end of the month. Some accounting databases will generate a report on this same basis.

There is no major difference in the category movements on each of the Cash Flow Statements prepared from either format as they both reconcile the opening cash balance with the ending cash balance with an explanation of where your cash has been invested during the period. There may however be slight differences in line elements due to changes in allocation of accounts to the Cash Flow Statements categories.

In my experience, the small business entrepreneur finds the direct format more informative.

Case Study—Format of Sam's Cash Flow Statement

Below is a copy of the Cash Flow Statement compiled under both the indirect and direct format for Sam's Landscaping & Design.

The indirect format is as follows.

Sam's Landscaping & Design

Cash Flow Statement

April 202X

Opening Cash Balance	**$37,361**
Cash Flow from Operating Activities	
Net Profit	$45,132
Accounts Receivable	$42,400
Accounts Payable	($39,049)
Tax Liabilities	$15,570
Payroll Liabilities	($11,429)
Visa - Credit Card	($1,437)
Net Cash Flows from Operating Activities	**$51,186**
Cash Flow from Investing Activities	
Plant & Equipment at Cost	($5,680)
Motor Vehicle at Cost	$0
Furniture & Fixtures at Cost	$0
Net Cash Flows from Investing Activities	($5,680)
Cash Flow from Financing Activities	
Loans	($4,611)
Drawings	($25,945)
Net Cash Flows from Financing Activities	($30,556)
Net Increase/Decrease for the period	**$14,950**
Closing Cash Balance	**$52,311**

The direct format is below.

Sam's Landscaping & Design

Cash Flow Statement
April 202X

Opening Cash Balance	**$37,361**
Cash Flow from Operating Activities	
Customer Cash Receipts	$275,272
Material Purchases	($127,558)
Labour Expenses	($39,064)
Plant & Equipment Expenses	$0
Motor Vehicle Expenses	($3,898)
Marketing Expenses	($2,694)
Building Expenses	($5,088)
Office Expenses	($4,870)
Professional Expenses	($1,160)
Finance Expenses	($1,591)
Credit Card Purchases	($5,797)
Taxes Paid	($32,137)
Net Cash Flows from Operating Activities	**$51,416**
Cash Flow from Investing Activities	
Plant & Equipment at Cost	($5,680)
Motor Vehicle at Cost	$0
Furniture & Fixtures at Cost	$0
Net Cash Flows from Investing Activities	**($5,680)**
Cash Flow from Financing Activities	
Loans	($4,841)
Capital Contributions	$0
Drawings	($25,945)
Net Cash Flows from Financing Activities	**($30,786)**
Net Increase/Decrease for the period	**$14,950**
Closing Cash Balance	**$52,311**

Sam compared the two Cash Flow Statements. He noticed the category balances between the two formats differed slightly. Debra explained this to be the interest paid on the loans. The direct format captured the loan repayment in full under financing activities, whereas the indirect format separated the interest from the loan repayments and included this in the net profit for the reporting period. The difference, she'd said, was immaterial because the value is insignificant.

Of the two formats, Sam preferred the direct method. He could see at a glance how much cash was being paid against his expenses and what he received from his customers regarding their invoices.

"What is the importance of the categories?"

"I'll start with the obvious, the opening cash balance."

Without cash, your SME cannot breathe. To understand how best to manage your cash and make the most of every dollar you earn, you not only need to generate a Cash Flow Statement every reporting period, but you will need to understand the elements that are reported on it and how they relate to one another.

Let's now look at the key elements of the Cash Flow Statement.

CHAPTER 8

The Ingredients of Oxygen

Elements of the Cash Flow Statement

THERE IS MORE to the Cash Flow Statement than opening and closing cash balances and a summation of deposits and withdrawals. We can extract this information directly from our bank statements. The Cash Flow Statement is designed to separate cash transactions into categories that explain what drives the cash flows in your SME and to help with decisions you make regarding the allocation of cash to particular activities. It will also serve in highlighting bad cash habits detrimental to your SME's survival.

From the bank statements you can make an assessment on whether your cash deposits exceed your cash withdrawals, whether your closing cash balance is high enough to cover next month's cash withdrawals, and verify what cash you hold at a specific date. However, from a cash management perspective, there is additional information provided by the Cash Flow Statement that can serve you.

The categories of the Cash Flow Statement group cash movements by their nature. Cash movements related to operational or day-to-day trading activities are consolidated. Expenditure and cash receipts related to investment in the infrastructure of your SME's business model are grouped together. Also, the source of finance and subsequent repayments that arise are reported together.

By separating our cash transactions into these three groups we can discern how much our normal operations contribute to our cash reserves, identify the funds required to grow our SMEs, and whether we are able to source funds for growth internally or externally to the business.

The Cash Flow Statement is as packed with information as the other two statements and can assist with:

- Understanding how much cash we source from within our business;
- Understanding the level of investment required from implemented growth strategies;
- Determining whether we can afford to finance our growth internally;
- Determine the impact of seeking funds external from third-parties;
- Determine whether we can afford to maintain debt;
- Understanding the effect combined operational and growth strategies have upon the cash balance;
- Determine whether your SME burns cash or accumulates it;
- Calculate how long cash reserves are likely to last;

- Building on and maintaining sufficient cash reserves.

The Cash Flow Statement, once understood, is an essential cash management tool that every business should be preparing, reading and analysing at the end of every month.

The five key elements of the Cash Flow Statement are:

- Opening Cash Balance;
- Net Cash from Operating Activities;
- Net Cash from Investing Activities;
- Net Cash from Financing Activities;
- Net Increase/Decrease in Cash Flow;
- Closing Cash Balance.

Opening Cash Balance

> ***Opening Cash Balance:*** *is the cash balance at the beginning of the reporting period.*

The Opening Cash Balance is effectively the Closing Cash Balance of the previous reporting period's Cash Flow Statement. It is also the closing total cash balance represented on the Balance Sheet at the end of the previous reporting period. The Cash Flow Statement is a flow statement, so to ensure no cash movements are missed, the following period should always begin the day after the last reporting period.

The Cash Flow Statement's Opening Cash Balance may represent the balance in your SME's bank account when you hold only one bank account. When your business holds more than one cash account, the total of all these cash accounts' opening balances will be summed to provide the Opening Cash Balance on your Cash Flow Statement.

The Cash Flow Statement reports on all cash transactions your SME undertakes, so all cash facilities used to manage cash transactions must be included in the opening cash balance. If your Balance Sheet totals all cash accounts, it is this total on the previous reporting period's Balance Sheet that is your opening cash balance for the current reporting period of the Cash Flow Statement.

The Opening Cash Balance is usually positioned at the head of the statement. Sometimes, it can be reported at the bottom of the statement before the closing cash balance.

Net Cash from Operating Activities

> ***Net Cash from Operating Activities****: captures all cash receipt and cash payment transactions undertaken in the normal course of day-to-day operations of the business.*

The Net Cash from Operating Activities is the summation of cash receipts, less cash payments applicable to the normal business activity. Cash receipts reflect the summation of all cash received regarding customer sales invoices. Cash payments represent the summation of cash paid regarding expenses detailed on the Profit & Loss Statement.

Operating activities will also include payments for obligations that may not necessarily be reported on the Profit & Loss Statement but are on the Balance Sheet, such as tax and payroll obligations. As tax and payroll obligations are a normal consequence of running a business, cash payments relating to them are included in the Net Cash Flow from Operating Activities.

In general, if a movement of cash is the result of normal day-to-day activity of your SME, it will be captured by the Net Cash from Operating Activities.

The importance of segmenting cash transactions applicable to your SME's operations is to determine what cash you are accumulating from your normal business activity. When Net Cash from Operating Activities is positive, it can finance the growth strategies your SME is implementing. When it is negative, you can determine how much additional cash you need to inject into your business to cover your normal business activities.

More often than not, Net Cash from Operating Activities is a positive figure which will be added to the Opening Cash Balance in the Cash Flow Statement.

Net Cash from Investing Activities

> ***Net Cash from Investing Activities:*** *all cash receipt and cash payment transactions that occur from investment activities.*

When a business is growing, it will usually need to upgrade its infrastructure and will experience increased business activity. Physical assets are purchased and overhead expenses increase. As business activity increases, so does the purchases of input costs like materials and labour. All this investment requires cash.

Sometimes investments may be made on items that are not necessarily utilised in their business, but are held for their investment value. For example, the purchase of shares and securities. These activities require cash, too.

There will also be a cash impact when divestment occurs. Divestment is a situation when revenue producing assets are sold or investments held for their value are exchanged for their market value. Both activities will cause cash to flow into the business.

Sometimes growth strategies cause an increase in day-to-day expenditures. Often this occurs up front before revenue is generated. When this expenditure affects operational activities, associated cash transactions will be included on the Cash Flow Statement under Net Cash from Operating Activities.

For entities experiencing aggressive growth, the Net Cash from Operating Activities often becomes negative. It is usually a temporary situation as cash receipts from boosted revenue streams will bring the net total back into a positive state.

Net Cash from Investing Activities captures growth activities outside the normal operations of the business. If purchasing or selling assets are not a normal trading activity, then they will be captured by the Cash Flow Statement under Net Cash from Investing Activities.

Asset sales will result in investment cash receipts and asset purchases will result in investment cash payments. Such cash transactions are summed in this section of the Cash Flow Statement to determine the Net Cash flow from Investing Activities.

More often than not, Net Cash from Investing Activities will be negative when a business is growing. When an SME is downsizing, it will be positive as assets are sold and cash flows into your business.

Net Cash from Financing Activities

Net Cash from Financing Activities: *all cash receipt and cash payment transactions related to financing activities.*

Financing activities refers to the sources of finance SME's access when they start up their entities, and finance investment decisions made later when their business activity grows. At start-up or during periods of growth, an SME often receives cash from the owner in the form of capital contributions. Alternatively, they may secure a business loan from a third-party external to the business.

Securing finance or bringing capital into the business will result in an injection of cash into the entity and is captured by the Cash Flow Statement under Net Cash from Financing Activities.

Subsequently, when cash is withdrawn from the business to repay business loans or for the personal benefit of the business owner in the form of drawings, this will result in a cash flow movement out of the entity. Such cash withdrawal transactions are captured by the Cash Flow Statement under Net Cash from Financing Activities.

More often than not, the Net Cash from Financing Activities will be negative. Whilst capital injections and business finance will cause a one-off cash inflow, the subsequent loan repayments and ongoing drawings will occur on a more regular basis.

Net Increase/Decrease in Cash Flow

> ***Net Increase/(Decrease) in Cash Flow:*** *is the summation of net cash from operating activities, net cash from investment activities and net cash from financing activities.*

The Net Increase/Decrease in cash flow is a calculation line like Gross Profit on the Profit & Loss Statement or Net Assets on the Balance Sheet. The net increase or decrease in the cash balance for the reporting period is represented on a single line so at a glance you can determine if you have increased your cash holdings or burned through cash for the designated reporting period.

The summation of the three categories of net cash flows on the Cash Flow Statement is also the difference between the Opening Cash Balance and Closing Cash Balance.

Net Increase/Decrease Cash Flows equals Net Operating Cash Flows plus Net Investing Cash Flows plus Net Financing Cash Flows

Net Increase/Decrease Cash Flows = Net Operating Cash Flows + Net Investing Cash Flows + Net Financing Cash Flows

The Net Increase/Decrease in cash flows is reported on the Cash Flow Statement after the three other categories and can be a positive or negative figure. If net cash flows are positive for the reporting period, more cash flowed in than went out of the business. If net cash flows are negative for the reporting period, more cash flowed out than came in.

Whilst we all prefer one over the other, Net Increase/Decrease in the cash flows line will rotate between cash flowing in and cash flowing out depending upon the spread of business activities during the reporting period.

Closing Cash Balance

Closing Cash Balance: *is the balance of your cash holdings on the last day of the reporting period.*

The Cash Flow Statement provides a summary of cash transactions that occurred during the reporting period to arrive at the closing balance reported on both statements. The Cash Flow Statement provides information on the ebbs and flows of cash movements specific to your SME, assisting you with managing your cash reserves and identifying where you are generating cash and spending cash.

On the Cash Flow Statement, the Closing Cash Balance is calculated by summing the Opening Cash Balance and the Net Increase/Decrease in cash flow.

Closing Cash Balance equals Opening Cash Balance plus Net Increase/Decrease Cash Flows

Closing Cash Balance = Opening Cash Balance + Net Increase/Decrease Cash Flows

The Closing Cash Balance will be the Opening Cash Balance reported on the Cash Flow Statement for the subsequent reporting period. At a glance, the reader can compare the opening and closing cash balances to make a quick assessment of whether cash reserves were increased during the reporting period or if cash was depleted and isolate the activities that drove that result.

Case Study—Where was Sam's Cash Going?

Sam eagerly examined the Cash Flow Statement for April as Debra explained the elements.

The opening balance was low. It took a hit in March when they purchased the block of land to house the equipment for the western suburbs team. Sam always preferred to see his bank balance around $75,000. It was no wonder they struggled to meet the payroll each month. They needed $40,000 to cover the full month's payroll, not thirty-five as he'd previously thought. He was going to have to watch that overtime.

Under net cash flow from operating activities, cash receipts totalled $275,000. He knew approximately $60,000 of that was from Thrifty Investments paying some of March's sales invoices early to boost what they paid out for the purchase of the land in March. He would benefit down the track with a team landscaping the properties Thrifty Investments were building, so it was merely *a timing issue. It also explained why now, in the middle of May, they were scrambling for cash.*

However, the net cash from operations was only $51,000. Debra explained that while about $30,000 was paid against old invoices, they were trying to catch up on and $32,000 was paid in taxes, net operating cash being positive was a good sign.

Sam's Landscaping & Design

Cash Flow Statement

April 202X

Opening Cash Balance	**$37,361**
Cash Flow from Operating Activities	
Customer Cash Receipts	$275,272
Material Purchases	($127,558)
Labour Expenses	($39,064)
Plant & Equipment Expenses	$0
Motor Vehicle Expenses	($3,898)
Marketing Expenses	($2,694)
Building Expenses	($5,088)
Office Expenses	($4,870)
Professional Expenses	($1,160)
Finance Expenses	($1,591)
Credit Card Purchases	($5,797)
Taxes Paid	($32,137)
Net Cash Flows from Operating Activities	**$51,416**
Cash Flow from Investing Activities	
Plant & Equipment at Cost	($5,680)
Motor Vehicle at Cost	$0
Furniture & Fixtures at Cost	$0
Net Cash Flows from Investing Activities	**($5,680)**
Cash Flow from Financing Activities	
Loans	($4,841)
Capital Contributions	$0
Drawings	($25,945)
Net Cash Flows from Financing Activities	**($30,786)**
Net Increase/Decrease for the period	**$14,950**
Closing Cash Balance	**$52,311**

Under investment activities, Sam found the cost of the wet saw, the tiller, and other power equipment they purchased so they wouldn't have to find cash for equipment hire. They also purchased an additional piece of each equipment to cover the western suburbs team starting in July.

Loan repayments, under financing activities, were also light at $5,000 Unfortunately, drawings at $26,000 were another glaring mark on what Debra called an "otherwise stable statement."

Only $15,000 was added to the cash balance during the month, and the closing balance of $52,000 was far from what they needed to meet their normal trading obligations, let alone repay Jake's loan and set up the new landscaping team. Debra clarified that once they implemented the cash initiatives they set from reviewing the P&L and Balance Sheet, net operating cash would increase and the movements of cash on this statement would stabilise. The key was to establish a rhythm between cash inflows and outflows.

The Cash Flow Statement is an instrumental tool in the SME's cash management strategy. The reconciliation of the opening and closing balances by separating the business activities into operating, investing and financing will allow the business owner to determine if they can finance growth initiatives from within the business, whether action needs to be taken regarding managing their operating cash levels and whether their drawings are at a level their SME's cash flow can afford.

Now that you are familiar with the elements of the Cash Flow Statement, we can look at defining what a healthy Cash Flow Statement would look like. Understanding the cash activities and how they relate to one another can go a long way in helping you improve your cash reserves.

CHAPTER 9

The Lifeline of your Entity

Without Cash Reserves, You Die!

NEED I SAY it again?

Cash is possibly the most important resource in your business, and it should be managed as such. I have always been a big believer that 'Money pays Respect'. When you manage your cash and the allocation of it with forethought, planning with a level of respect regarding the consequences of where and when you spend it, cash will naturally accumulate in your bank account.

Cash reserves are vital to business success.

Part of the cash management strategies you implement will include determining the optimal level of cash reserves for your SME. A cash reserve is the level of cash you retain in your business as a safety net. It is like nest egg savings for a household.

From time to time there will be unforeseen problems that will drain on your cash reserves. Occasionally, an external event could have a detrimental impact on your revenue streams and subsequently dry up the inflow of cash, requiring you to draw on your SME's cash savings.

The astute business owner will set aside a level of cash to be held in reserve that will facilitate their day-to-day business activity when a crisis befalls them. The level of cash reserves your business requires to manage these unforeseen circumstances is as specific and as individual as your SME is.

The big question is, how do you get your business in a position to accumulate enough cash to maintain a safety level of cash reserves when there is not enough to grow your business, to pay you a wage or possibly not enough to pay the day-to-day expenses?

Generating a Profit & Loss Statement and a Balance Sheet at the end of each reporting period is not enough to ensure you have enough cash for your SME to breathe. Whilst profit plays a large part in contributing to your available cash flow, the information on the Profit & Loss Statement falls short of reflecting your entire cash situation. The Balance Sheet provides an assessment of the liquidity of your assets and their ability to meet your debts and obligations, but fails to clearly communicate the whole story of where your cash is allocated during a reporting period.

By preparing a Cash Flow Statement with a Profit & Loss Statement and a Balance Sheet, you put yourself in a position to understand and better manage the flows of cash through your entity. Strategic management of your cash flows that increase your operating cash, remove cash trapped on the Balance Sheet, streamline payment of debts and obligations, and grow the equity you hold in your business will see increased net cash flow into your business and take up residence in your bank account.

The Cash Flow Statement summarises the information provided on the other two statements in the context of your total cash resources. It will highlight the cash generating activities and those business activities that drain the cash from your bank account. By understanding where your cash is coming from and where it is going, you can highlight behaviours that boost your cash balance and those that are sabotaging your ability to grow or meet daily commitments.

The Cash Flow Statement tells you the whole cash story. It can provide you with gems of information that assist you with changing behaviours and implementing strategies to improve the management of your cash.

When your Cash Flow Statement is healthy, your business will generate enough cash to establish your optimal level of cash reserves, whilst being able to meet daily commitments, grow your business and still have enough to pay yourself.

Defining a Healthy Cash Flow Statement

A healthy Cash Flow Statement for your SME will be specific to your desired cash reserves level, the growth initiatives you have in place and how you intend to finance them, and your ability to generate positive operating cash flows. Each activity on the statement needs to be assessed in relationship to the others to fully grasp what cash your SME needs to be sustainable and to grow.

If we presume that the opening cash balance is at your desired cash reserve level, then you will want to ensure the cash inflows and cash outflows reported on your Cash Flow Statement, at a minimum, negate to zero. When this occurs, you are maintaining your cash safety net and all the cash coming into your business is enough to meet all your outgoing cash commitments. No cash drain on your cash balance occurs, and the integrity of your Cash Flow Statement can be maintained.

When your opening cash balance is below your desired cash reserve level and your aim is to increase it, you will need to manage your cash inflows and outflows to ensure they add to your cash balance and result in a closing cash balance that is higher than the opening balance. The same cash strategies would need to be applied to each subsequent reporting period until you reach your desired cash reserve level. The Cash Flow Statement would show improvement in your cash holdings and be considered moving in a healthy direction.

If your opening cash balance is in excess of your desired cash reserve level and your cash inflows and outflows add further to the cash balance, you can say your cash flow statement is healthy. However, when your cash reserves are excessive and continue to be increased through normal trading, then you can say you are not utilising your cash resources effectively and are missing out on growth or investment opportunities. While the Cash Flow Statement could be considered healthy from an operational perspective, it would not be from an investment point of view.

Regarding the activities reported on the Cash Flow Statement, each can also be assessed individually.

Normal operational activities are healthy when they are generating a positive net cash flow. Positive net cash flows mean you have funds available to invest in your business and to meet any financial obligations. You are also giving your business a good chance of adding to your cash reserves, subject to the level of investing and financing activities. Whilst there will be occasions when net operating cash flow will be negative because of expected seasonal trends or due to deliberate and managed trading growth, as long as the long-term net operating cash flows are positive, you are in a healthy operating cash position.

Net cash flows from investing activities will be negative more often than not. Negative cash flows regarding investing should not be seen as detrimental to your business. It is a positive sign that your business is growing. When you ensure cash flows from investing activities are within the reach of meeting your operational commitments and obligations, or you secure affordable finance, a negative net cash flow from investing activities is a healthy position.

While it is unusual, net cash flows from investing activities can be positive. When positive on a recurring basis, it is usually a sign of downsizing your business when revenue producing assets are sold for cash. As long as this is a controlled strategy, there is no concern. If not, and it is ongoing, you should be wary of the impact on future revenue. With fewer assets, revenue and associated cash receipts will be reduced and so too will be your operating cash.

When growth and investment require it, net cash flows from financing activities may be positive due to additional funds sourced through business loans or from capital contributions from the owner. This situation would be considered healthy as long as the resulting repayment instalments are not absorbing all the operational net cash. It is a sign that your business is growing. However, if your business is not growing and net cash flows from financing activities are consistently higher than net operating cash flows, it indicates you are too highly geared or possibly the level of drawings is more than the business can afford.

From this discussion, you will have developed an appreciation that the Cash Flow Statement and the cash flows in and out of your SME are considerably sophisticated.

Once you have developed an appreciation of the sophistication and gems of information the Cash Flow Statement provides, you can assess the integrity of your cash situation and the health of the statement.

Below, I have drafted a broad and general outline of what would be considered a healthy position for each of the Cash Flow Statement's elements in a perfect world. Note the element's status depends on the other elements and whether or not your entity is growing.

Healthy Status of the Cash Flow Statement	
Element	**Healthy Position**
Opening Cash Balance	Optimal Cash Reserve Level.
Net Cash from Operating Activities	Positive cash flows > investing cash flows & financing cash flows. Growth – temporary negative cash flows. No Growth – positive cash flows.
Net Cash from Investing Activities	Growth – Negative cash flows less than operating cash flows and financing cash flows No Growth – No cash flows. Downsizing - Positive cash flows.
Net Cash from Financing Activities	Growth – Positive cash flows. No Growth – negative cash flows less than operating cash flows.
Net Increase/Decrease Cash Flow	No Growth – Positive net cash flows. Growth – Temporarily negative, with the expectation that increase cash receipts from operations will be generated in the near future. Growth – Positive with cash receipts from financing activities covering the subsequent investment.
Closing Cash Balance	Optimal Cash Reserve level

Drawings on the Cash Flow Statement

When we assessed the affordable level of drawings your SME could sustain on the Balance Sheet, we mentioned making a similar assessment on the Cash Flow Statement.

Drawings are reported on the Cash Flow Statement under financing activities. As they are the opposite of capital contributions to the business, they are represented here to signify a reduction in the cash balance due to drawings on the SME's equity.

A similar assessment of an affordable level of drawings can be made on the Cash Flow Statement. Your level of drawings should not be more than thirty percent of net cash from operating activities. When it is, you are withdrawing cash that could repay third-party finance or more importantly, cash you can reinvest into your SME through the purchase of assets and expanding your business activity. It is reasonable to expect that seventy percent of the business' cash should be sufficient for a reasonable level of growth, repaying the instalments of a past loan and meeting the next month's operating cash commitments.

If you are fortunate enough to have earnings and operating cash that facilitate more than what you reasonably require to survive personally, then the threshold of affordable drawings should be held at only what you require. When the thirty percent of net cash from operating activities is in excess of thirty percent of your current earnings, then the lower of the two should set your drawings threshold. If thirty percent of your current earnings is lower than thirty percent of your net cash from operating activities, then again, the lower of the two should be your drawings threshold.

The more funds you retain in your business the better, and drawings at all times should be limited by what you need to survive financially personally and only what your business can afford. Once money has been withdrawn from your business, it is no longer available for your business to benefit from and is effectively gone forever.

Optimal Cash Reserves

Before you can assess the health of your SME's Cash Flow Statement, you need to determine your optimal cash reserve. This is the amount of cash that would serve as a safety net should your business activity be negatively impacted unexpectedly. Most small businesses operate with cash reserves that would last twenty-eight days. Under this scenario, an SME will be operating from one month to the next as an employee that is living from payslip to payslip.

It is unlikely that your business could recover from a severe impact caused by an external event like a natural disaster or an economic downturn within twenty-eight days. In some cases, it can take months or even years to return to normal trading levels. To maintain a cash balance, you could survive on for several years is unrealistic and a misuse of your cash resources during boom periods. However, it is reasonable and prudent to put aside enough cash to cover several months of trading and buy you time as you pivot your business.

Usually when these unforeseeable impacts occur, revenue streams and therefore cash receipts will not dry up entirely, so a cash reserve that would last three months without cash receipts would support you for a longer period depending upon the rate you burn through your cash. A three-month level of cash is a respectable level of savings you can strive towards and maintain, yet it is likely to support your business for much longer.

You need to decide on the optimal level of cash reserves you would like to maintain as a safety net for your SME. A person who has low levels of risk aversion may be more than comfortable maintaining only a month's worth of cash requirements. Those at the other end of the spectrum with high levels of risk aversion may prefer a twelve-month safety net.

If you are in an industry that is relatively stable from one month to the next, your optimal cash reserves may only be a couple of months, but in industries where there are seasonal implications that cause great fluctuations in business activity from one month to the next, six or twelve months of cash reserves may be preferred.

It is a fine line determining the optimum level of cash reserves you desire and what your SME can hope to achieve and maintain. However, one thing is for certain, without cash reserves your business will struggle to offset sudden and significant downturns in revenue streams long-term.

I operate my own SME with a three-month level of cash reserves. I base my calculation on the cash flows associated with maintaining my business model. That is Overhead Expenses as reported on the Profit & Loss Statement and cash outflows on the Balance Sheet regarding financing obligations, growth requirements and an affordable level of drawings. Cost of sales items I have excluded from this calculation for these expenses rise and fall in line with revenue. If I have no revenue, it is reasonable to assume that there will be no cost of sale expenses.

I have measured the cash outflows of my business model by preparing a direct format Cash Flow Statement for a twelve-month reporting period. Isolating and summing all the relevant cash outflows, I calculate the average cash outflows per month and multiply this by three. This calculation provides me with the level of cash I would require to survive a three-month period where I would not receive cash receipts and still be able to cover my overheads and financial cash payments.

Optimal Cash Balance equals Overhead Expenses plus Investing Activities Cash Outflow plus Financing Activities Cash Outflow divided by twelve multiplied by three

Optimal Cash Balance = (Overhead Expenses + Investing Activities Cash Outflow + Financing Activities Cash Outflow) /12 x 3

You may be surprised by how much cash flows out of your business in a three-month period. However, this exercise will educate you on what cash your SME would need if revenue streams disappeared. While I strive to maintain a three-month safety net from one month to the next, occasionally it is above this level and more often than not it will fall below this threshold. When it falls below, I strive to increase the balance through positive net cash inflows until it is once again at or above this level. It is a constant juggling act.

The health of the Cash Flow Statement is determined by a balance of the three cash flow activities and maintaining the desired level of cash reserves. Constant and strategic cash management is required to keep the cash flows of your SME in check. Review of the Cash Flow Statement in conjunction with the Profit & Loss Statement and Balance Sheet at the conclusion of each month will help guide you to keep your cash position in a healthy state.

Case Study—The Health of Sam's Cash Flow

"Overall, your Cash Flow Statement is solid. You have positive operating cash and the cash drain from third-party loans is light, even if we take into account the likely repayment on the refinancing loan. Your cash problem comes from not only the high level of drawings, but how fast you're growing and that you're endeavouring to finance this internally. By limiting the level of drawings and making the other changes we discussed regarding the Profit & Loss Statement and Balance Sheet, you should see a quick turnaround in your cash position."

"May is tight," Sam highlighted with regret.

"Yes, because one of your builders paid early, and you're playing catch up with some supplier invoices. When I say a quick turnaround, I mean that it will take three to six months after changes have been implemented, and you'll need to keep in check what you're spending regarding your new revenue streams. Gradually, things will improve and by reviewing the Cash Flow Statement each month, and you will see the impact and capitalise upon it, making your cash work harder for you."

"Good."

"Now we need to decide what level of cash reserves you would like to have. I usually work on three months, which for your business is in the vicinity of $169,000."

"That much?"

"If you had that balance in your account now, you'd be able to meet this month's cash outflows. Wouldn't that feel good?"

Sam could only nod.

"We can make it two months if you prefer, but if you keep needing to set up entire landscape teams who are fully equipped at the outset, you'll need reserves to finance it. The alternative is to borrow."

"The more we can finance internally, the better. I'll be happy if it's only the vehicle we need to finance. If cash is going to be available like you say, we can pay for the digger and other equipment internally."

Debra showed Sam and Beth an additional report she prepared. "From this table you can assess where you are and where you would ideally like to be regarding the Cash Flow Statement. These are monthly figures. Once you are more comfortable reading and managing the cash flows in and out, we can look at annual targets."

Sam and Beth studied the table.

Sam's Landscaping & Design - Cash Flow Targets

Element	Target	Actual
Optimal Cash Reserves	$168,994	$52,311
Net Cash from Operating Activities	$75,000	$51,416
Net Cash from Investing Activities	($20,000)	($5,680)
Net Cash from Financing Activities	($14,500)	($30,786)
Net Increase/(Decrease) in Cash Flows	$ 40,500	$ 14,950

"In consideration of our earlier discussions and your probable increased business activity, your operating cash will increase significantly. I've estimated it at $75,000. We can adjust it down the track if need be.

"I've assumed an average target of $20,000 per month for setting up and equipping the new team, as I recall you mentioned each team required about a $100,000 investment and some of this you've already spent. Taking into account the adjusted level of drawings and the refinancing loan, you'll need around $15,000 for financing activities.

"I think it is reasonable to assume you can add approximately $40,000 to your cash balance each month. Taking into account your growth, investing cash may blow out a little from time to time, but you should reach your optimal cash reserves in about six months."

"That sounds too good to be true," Sam said.

They further discussed what needed to be put into place to have the western suburbs team established, generating revenue by July and positive cash flows by August. They revisited some of the strategies they discussed earlier regarding the Profit & Loss Statement and Balance Sheet and how they would specifically impact the Cash Flow Statement and the cash balance.

Overall, Sam was relieved there was hope. Paul was right; meeting with Debra was more than worth the time.

Debra told them she would discuss the statements she had prepared with Frank, if the bank required his endorsement. They came to an agreement that she would visit them once a month to prepare and review the three core financial statements with them, and would focus on keeping them on track whilst they grew familiar with analysing the reports and using them to manage their business.

"Will it take as long each time?" Sam asked, concerned the exercise had taken most of the day.

"Next time it'll only be a few hours. In a couple of months, we'll get it down to about an hour each month, I promise."

Unfortunately, we don't live in a perfect world and as most small business struggle with managing their cash flow, their Cash Flow Statement will most likely be far from stable. But there is hope.

The purpose of the Cash Flow Statement is to educate you on the flows of cash through your business and guide you in how to improve your cash balance. By preparing and generating a Cash Flow Statement regularly, you can make an assessment of where your cash is going. The objective of categorising cash flows into operational, investing and financing activities will clarify where you are allocating your cash, allow you to assess the benefits and disadvantages of doing so, make decisions to drive cash expenditure in the most profitable and cash savvy activities, and to identify when you need to seek external finance to support your growth initiatives.

Without a Cash Flow Statement, the SME is flying blind.

Below is a list of all the things you should now know about the Cash Flow Statement:

- The purpose of the Cash Flow Statement is to identify where your cash is being allocated;
- The Cash Flow Statement is divided into three business activities : Operating Activities, Investing Activities and Financing Activities;
- Net cash from operating activities captures cash inflows and outflows associated with normal trading activities;
- Net cash for operating activities encompasses cash generated from the Profit & Loss Statement, cash flows associated with current assets and current liabilities on the Balance Sheet;
- Net cash flow from operating activities is usually positive;

- Net cash from investing activities captures cash inflows and outflows associated with downsizing or growing your business assets;
- Net cash from investing activities encompasses cash transactions associated with purchasing non-current assets on the Balance Sheet;
- Net cash from investing activities is usually negative, particularly if your business is growing;
- Net cash from financing activities captures cash inflows and outflows associated with third-party finance or capital contributions or drawings of the business owner;
- Net cash from financing activities encompasses transactions associated with non-current liabilities and equity elements of the Balance Sheet;
- Net cash from financing activities is usually negative, but may be positive when the business is growing;
- Net increase/decrease in cash flows is the summation of net cash flows from operating, investing and financing activities;
- Net increase/decrease in cash flows will add/deduct from your opening cash balance;
- Opening cash balance is the closing cash balance of the last reporting period;
- Closing cash balance is the opening cash balance plus net increase/decrease in cash flows;
- Opening and closing cash balances should be maintained at the optimal cash reserve level;

- The optimal cash reserve level is the cash balance you have determined as being a sustainable and sufficient safety net;
- Drawings should be at or below thirty percent of your net cash flows from operating activities;
- The lower of thirty percent of net cash flows from operating activities and thirty percent of current earnings should be the threshold for an affordable level of drawings;
- Changing behaviour habits associated with the three business activities will result in changes to the net cash flows of your entity;
- Cash management strategies should include defining an optimal level of cash reserves, maximising net cash flows from operating activities and balancing net cash flows from investing activities and financing activities to enable maintenance of the optimal cash balance.

Part 3

Fine Tuning Your Finance Engine

Case Study
Sam's Dilemma Solved

SIX MONTHS PASSED *since Sam received the fateful call from his brother-in-law. The shackles his business imprisoned him with loosened every month until they finally fell away. Sam no longer stressed over an empty bank account or where he would find the money to pay the month's obligations. He gets a full night's sleep every night, sleeping as peacefully as his wife had six months ago.*

He is in more control of his business than he ever has been. Sam gained an intimate insight into the finances of his business, and now thoroughly understands how his decisions impact his profit and cash levels. With each passing day, he is another step further in maximising the benefits he can gain from a well-run Finance Engine.

Debra, their business coach, helped with the refinance for Jake's loan. She worked closely with Frank on their behalf as part of her monthly fee, explaining the measures she implemented regarding the preparation of the financial statements, and the strategies Sam was implementing into his business. Sam was floored when he received an invoice from Frank that was significantly lower than what he'd been paying previously.

When the bank's funds came through, he cried with relief.

Sam would never forget the look on Jake's face when they met for beers and he told Jake the loan repayment was transferred to him earlier that day. To witness Jake's surprise and liberation was worth every penny.

Solving the loan dilemma was not the only impact Debra had on their business.

Debra spent considerable time with Beth after their initial meeting, training her on how to ensure all transactions were captured weekly by their accounting software and how to reconcile it at the end of each month so the statements generated were correct. Each month they got together and reviewed the statements.

The review was a lengthy exercise for the first few months as it took time to become familiar with what the statements were reporting. However, the past month's meeting only took just over an hour to go over the impact of their decisions and what further changes they wanted to make. Using the tables to assess the health of their statements proved invaluable for saving time, as they only sourced the full statement when activity fell short or was markedly improved.

Overall, their profitability levels increased by five percent and the gross profit margin hovered around forty percent for the past two months. They consistently have cash in their bank account, and Sam better understands the financial implications of his decisions and where his cash is going. The results were the direct efforts of several initiatives.

Sam immediately increased the mark-up on private residential projects to fifty percent, ensuring all costs were captured. He secured prior agreement from clients to accept a five percent increase on the initial quote and when the initial project was complete, updated quotes were provided and agreed to before commencing the additional activity.

Discounts were avoided when additional value could be provided and Sam put a stop to discounted jobs for his mates for the time being.

They even altered the working roaster so all employees with special skills were dedicated to private and more lucrative residential projects for at least three weeks of the month, reducing the cost incurred on builder's jobs and reworks. Overtime was kept to a minimum and only allowed on weekend jobs.

Sam made a commitment to raising invoices the day jobs were completed, allowing payment to be due and received a few days earlier than if he invoiced only at the end of the week or month. They implemented a collection process which brought in all past due account receivables, kept on top of the balance payments of new invoices, and ensured that a thirty percent deposit was received on new residential projects before materials were ordered and the job commenced.

Sam spoke with several of their major suppliers and negotiated credit terms, which allowed them to reduce the use of credit cards and streamline the payment process. Debra conducted an analysis to determine the best day for issuing the supplier payments based on their credit terms and cash flow. The angry and frustrated calls requesting immediate payments were a thing of the past.

They no longer ran personal expenses through the business and had been paid wages every month since June. Beth even had Debra advise on how best to manage their household finances, and she provided a few tips that made it easier to meet commitments.

The greatest achievement, from Sam's perspective, was when they financed a fully equipped landscape team for the western suburbs from their own cash. The only exception being the new truck. They used a shipping container as an office, located on the land they purchased the previous March, while they waited for council permits. They would build a small hut, big enough for one desk to serve as their future office. Beth and Debra would work from their current site in the eastern suburbs.

They had not quite reached their optimal cash balance due to the investment in equipment and the new team, however, they were only $40,000 shy at the end of October. They always had funds to cover weekly payroll, which was an incredible relief. Sam also suspected that Thrifty Investments were happy not to have to pay their invoices early every month.

Despite the extent of financial benefits, they weren't the only positives to come out of this exercise.

Sam's relationship with his workers drastically improved. Onsite camaraderie developed, and they were not only completing the jobs sooner, but the improved quality meant few reworks were required. Sam spent less time yelling and more time speaking with them about life outside of the job. Every second Friday afternoon, they held a barbecue and threw back a few beers. At first, only a few of the boys hung around, but they were all there the past two Fridays and one brought along a mate who asked Sam if he would consider him the next time he was employing.

Beyond that, Sam's relationship with his kids also improved. He dedicated his weekends to running them around for sporting activities and staying to watch whenever he could, rather than escaping to finish pressing jobs. Max, his eldest, sought him out more often when he was home, whilst Tyler and Oakley would spend hours clambering all over him, grateful that he didn't push them away or scowl at them for interrupting.

Sam learned that Oakley's favourite colour was yellow and his favourite toy was Leroy, the teddy he received from his grandmother when he was born.

Beth appreciated the support and they rarely fought anymore. Communication improved over time, and they were rebuilding the damage wrought by the last few years. Sam was grateful their relationship was returning to a level of normalcy. She still met with her girlfriends for lunch, however it was now only occasionally, not three times a week like before. Sam also found time to catch up with his own mates, rather than seeing them on the fly or when they called him for landscaping work.

Managing his business was no longer the torture it had been. Life was good. Not only had his business found financial freedom, but he found wellbeing and peace within himself.

Change Your Financial Destiny

Like Sam, you too can gain full control of your SME's Finance Engine and achieve financial freedom for your business and yourself.

Every business has a Finance Engine and it should be seen and nurtured by the business owner as an asset and not a burden that must be addressed to satisfy statutory and taxation requirements. You and your wellbeing are the most important reasons to have a well-managed Finance Engine and all it takes is some investment in understanding the flows of finance specific to your business, and how this knowledge can improve your management and shore up the chances of success for your business.

Grasping an understanding of what constitutes your SME's Finance Engine is just the first step. The three core financial statements—Profit & Loss Statement, Balance Sheet and Cash Flow Statement—provide the results of your business activity, but it is the who, why, how and when that will determine how well your SME's Finance Engine runs.

Every SME should prepare a Cash Flow Statement on a monthly basis at minimum. However, from what you have learned about the Profit & Loss Statement and Balance Sheet and the gems of information they can provide, warrant that the three core financial statements should be prepared and reviewed regularly.

We clarified that the entrepreneur's sole responsibility is to manage and drive their SME's business activity by reading and understanding the three core financial statements. By allocating the responsibility of preparing your SME's books to a qualified bookkeeper, you can ensure that not only the tasks of data entry occur, but your books are fully reconciled. The integrity of the three core financial statements your Finance Engine generates is maintained, allowing you to make confident decisions about day-to-day operations, growing strategies and how you intend to achieve your vision.

Profits are not the only element in your business that affects your cash flow. By interrogating the three core financial statements you can isolate how to influence your SME's profitability, understand how much your business model costs to run, improve your levels of liquidity by releasing trapped cash, make decisions about whether to finance the growth of your entity internally or by third-party finance, and know how much you can be paid by your business. All are good reasons to invest in getting your Finance Engine maintained like any other asset of your SME.

Throwing all your purchase receipts and bank statements into a shoe box to ship off to your tax accountant at the end of the financial year is no longer enough in our constantly changing environment. By investing in accounting software to capture your business transactions, you can efficiently reconcile your SME's data and generate the three core financial statements that meet the criteria for effective statements: timely, accurately and consistently.

The question of when you should, not only address the regularity of preparing and reviewing the three core finance statements, but also when you should take the leap to invest in yourself and your business to fine tune your SME's Finance Engine and reclaim financial control of your business. It is never too early or too late to learn about the purpose of the three core financial statements, their elements, the relationship of elements within each statement and the relationship of each statement with the other two.

When the what, who, why, how, and when have been defined for your business, you are set to review the three core financial statements.

The Profit & Loss Statement with the three levels of profit can guide you on when you should increase your business activity and volume of sales or adjusting your selling price and/or input costs to improve the bottom line of net profit. It is also a key influencer of the operating cash generated by your business, cash that is used to invest and finance your SME.

The Balance Sheet encapsulates your SME's financial stability by summarising the held and accessible resources of your business model. It can provide nuggets of information on your ability to meet day-to-day debts and obligations, identify cash that can become trapped and explain why it is not in your bank account, highlight the claim third-parties have over your business assets, and determine how much you can be paid.

The Cash Flow Statement breaks down your business activities into operating, investing and financing activities, allowing you to identify which activities generate cash and which activities burn through your cash. It allows you to identify the behaviours that are key drivers of your cash flow, facilitating decisions that improve net cash inflows and optimise cash balances your SME has immediate access to.

Only with all three core financial statements can you truly get the full picture of the financial flows your business generates, allowing you to optimise each dollar invested in your business activity to generate more profits, more cash and financial freedom.

With all this valuable information at your fingertips, shouldn't you get cracking and start today?

This brings us to the end of the *Discover Your Finance Engine* self-help guide, however it should only be the beginning of your journey. You should now be able to realise the asset your Finance Engine can be, establish a financial summary of your business that can be reviewed in an hour per month, improve the intimate knowledge of your entity and optimise your cash balance.

Thank you for investing in this self-help guide. I hope it has improved your knowledge of your SME's Finance Engine and the three core financial statements it can generate.

If you are interested in the next steps regarding educating yourself about your Finance Engine, please keep reading until you have turned the last page.

Bibliography

Australian Accounting Standards Board, March 2020, "AASB 1060 General Purpose Financial Statements – Simplified Disclosures for For-Profit and Not-for-Profit Tier 2 Entities", https://www.aasb.gov.au/admin/file/content105/c9/ACCED295_08-19.pdf (19th August 2019): Australian Government.

Chartered Professional Accountants Canada, 2015, "Accounting Standards for Private Enterprise, CPA Canada Handbook – Accounting", 2015 ed, Toronto Canada: CPA, Chartered Professional Accountants of Canada. https://www.worldcat.org/title/cpa-canada-handbook-accounting/oclc/901016611

CPA Australia Ltd, 2014, "Managing Cash Flows – Learning Manual", Southbank VIC Australia: CPA Australia.

Federal Accounting Standards Advisory Board (FASAB), June 30, 2018, "FASAB Handbook of Federal Accounting Standards and Other Pronouncements, as Amended", 17th ed, http://files.fasab.gov/pdffiles/2018_fasab_handbook.pdf (24th June 2020)

John Hoggett, Lew Edwards, et al., 7th January 2003, "Accounting in Australia", 5th Edition, Milton Qld Australia: John Wiley & Sons.

International Accounting Standards Board (IASB), 2015, "IFRS For SMEs", 2015, London UK: International Accounting Standards Board. https://www.ifrs.org/issued-standards/ifrs-for-smes/

Donald E Kieso Ph.D. CPA, Jerry J Weygandt Ph.D. CPA, Terry D Warfield, 4th April 2016, "Intermediate Accounting", 16th ed, Milton Qld Australia: John Wiley & Sons.

Acknowledgements

To my son, thank you for your silent support and for being so forgiving for all those nights we ate at all hours, because I had to finish up one more paragraph. I hope I have shown by example that your dreams are never out of your reach.

To my parents, Gerda and William, thank you for installing in me an adventurous spirit and for raising me to be a problem solver. I am so grateful for your unfailing support and for being my greatest champions.

I would like to thank the staff at Author Academy Elite, for without their program and accompanying coaching this book would have been relegated to my pile of unpublished manuscripts and have never reached the printer.

In particular: Abigail Young for inspiring me to write the case study in fiction. It was just the thing to lighten the mood of what can be a very dry and boring topic. Nanette O'Neal, Tony Colsen and Daphne Smith for your contributions and suggestions on the subtitle that seemed to keep eluding me. For Kary Oberbrunner for creating Author Academy Elite and inspiring authors across the world to live their dream.

I also wish to thank all the people associated with Igniting Souls, a tribe associated with Author Academy Elite. Without the safety net you provide, the always available resourceful pool of guidance, support and direction this book would never have been published.

I would like to thank Gino Wickman not only for the testimonial but also for your kind and encouraging words.

I also wish to thank my editor, Diana James. Your efforts of removing additional unnecessary words, streamlining sentence structure and tempering my flowery efforts to communicate my message have transformed my manuscript into this masterpiece.

Finally, to all the business owners and executives I have worked with during the past twenty-five plus years. This book is the accumulation of only some of the experiences and challenges we faced together. The knowledge about managing cash in the small business would have fallen far short of what this book required, without what we learned together.

About the Author

Debra Cooper is an author, coach, and small business owner with the desire to empower other small business owners with intellectual knowledge about their entities and provide customised solutions that make small business management a breeze. She is a qualified CPA with a Master in Business Administration who lives with her family in the southeastern suburbs of Melbourne, Australia.

About

Zephyr Management Solutions is a small business in the southeastern suburbs of Melbourne, Australia, of which Debra Cooper is the owner and founder. She provides small business management solutions to empower small and medium business owners to overcome the challenges on the entrepreneurial journey. With a focus on finances and how they flow through an entity, solutions are delivered by self-help guides, group coaching, one-on-one coaching, and courses. Topics include finances, business development, and strategic management.

Zephyr Management Solutions - making small business management a breeze.

zephyrms.com

About

bizzness breeze essentials

'bizzness breeze essentials' is a FREE private group of Zephyr Management Solutions.

As a member of the group, you will have access to additional content to support your journey in *Discover Your Finance Engine*.

If you are an aspiring or active business owner, who is…

- Supportive of fellow business owners
- Not averse to taking action
- Sees opportunity in adversity
- Interested in improving management of your business
- Willing to learn and grow

… then I would love for you to join 'bizzness breeze essentials'.

Together, we make small business management a *breeze*.

zephyrms.com/community

1:1 Coaching

Zephyr Management Solutions can assist with your journey to discover your SME's "Finance Engine" by providing one-on-one coaching with the author, *Debra Cooper*.

Debra will partner with you, providing guidance on the cash generating formula of your business, how to manage the resulting cash flows and help define implementable strategies to fine tune your SME's "Finance Engine".

zephyrms.com/coaching

Coming in 2021!

Discover your Finance Engine—the Course

...is an online course that will assist you in...

- Developing a customised process to preparing effective financial statements
- Identifying the importance of your SME's three core financial statements
- Understanding the elements of your SME's financial statements
- Identifying which elements consume and trap cash
- Setting reachable customised targets to build a sustainable SME

zephyrms.com/academy

Coming in 2021!

The 2nd book in the "Finance Engine" series.

"Deep Dive into your Finance Engine"

With a focus upon financial risk, we take a look behind the face-value of the three core financial statements and how to mitigate your business' exposure.

zephyrms.com/library

More information can be found at ...

zephyrms.com

Made in the USA
Las Vegas, NV
10 September 2023

77385411R00148